Saved from the Sea

A collection of fourteen true stories, this book is a tribute to the bravery of lifeboat crews, divers and pilots who have saved lives from the sea. It is also an amazing account of people shipwrecked, adrift at sea or trapped under the water, from the boy and his father attacked by sharks on their small raft to the passengers and crew of an ocean liner, cast away on a desert coastline. They all fought hard for survival, and their experiences make gripping reading.

John Davies became a journalist after serving in the Royal Navy during the war. He is the author of numerous articles and books, both fiction and non-fiction, and lives in London.

D1798194

SAVED FROM THE SEA

John Davies

Illustrated by John Glover

Beaver Books

First published in 1977 by
The Hamlyn Publishing Group Limited
London · New York · Sydney · Toronto
Astronaut House, Feltham, Middlesex, England

© Copyright Text John Davies 1977
© Copyright Illustrations
The Hamlyn Publishing Group Limited 1977
ISBN 0 600 38239 7

Printed in England by Cox and Wyman Limited
London, Reading and Fakenham
Set in Monotype Imprint

Contents

The Singing Submarine

The tiny underwater craft lay crippled deep down on the ocean bed, 250 kilometres from the nearest land. Nearly 500 metres above it a freshening wind was whipping up the surface of the grey, heaving Atlantic to gale conditions.

At the depth at which the casualty lay, all was quiet except for the sound that was coming from the little submarine. Under the circumstances, it was a very strange sound indeed – the sound of singing.

There were two men in the submarine, Roger Chapman and Roger Mallinson, and they had been singing on and off for hours. Not just for the fun of it, nor even to keep their spirits up, but because their very lives might well depend upon it.

They were trying to make it easier for rescuers using sound location apparatus to locate them. A sustained sound is easier to pick up with such apparatus than an intermittent noise such as banging. So the two Rogers sang.

The midget sub was called *Pisces III*. It was an appropriate name since Pisces is Latin for fish, and *Pisces III*, less than six metres long, wasn't really any bigger than, say, certain species of shark.

Pisces III weighed eleven tonnes and could dive to a maximum depth of 900 metres. She could stay underwater for seventy-two hours.

That period of time had now taken on a terrifying significance.

The little submarine's plight was the result of an accident that had happened in the very early hours of Wednesday, 19th August, 1973. That meant the two men stranded on the ocean bed must be rescued at the latest by roughly the same time on the Saturday of that week. An hour or two after that could be too late.

What was *Pisces III* doing when the accident befell her? She belonged to Vickers Oceanics Ltd, a firm specialising in underwater work, and she had been playing an important part in the laying of a new trans-Atlantic telephone cable. The cable, costing some £30 million, would be able to carry no fewer than 1840 telephone calls at the same time, which was more than all the existing cables put together.

On the Continental Shelf – the comparatively shallow waters within 150 kilometres or so of land – the cable had to be protected from damage by the trawls of fishing vessels, and that was where *Pisces III* came in. Her job was to bury the cable by digging a trench in the ocean bed with high-pressure water jets and a specially designed mechanical claw. When a section of the trench had been dug, she pushed the cable into it.

It was a big job for such a tiny vessel. *Pisces III* was scheduled to bury a total of sixty kilometres of cable at an average rate of two kilometres per day. Allowing for rest periods and minor hold-ups, she would be on the job for something like forty days.

As it happened, her work had been brought to a sudden and dramatic halt after not much more than half that time.

The job was being carried out off the south-west coast of Ireland, and the two-man sub had been brought out there from Dover aboard the *Vickers Voyager*, a big fishing trawler which had been specially converted to lower and haul up *Pisces III* in pretty well any weather conditions.

For over three weeks all went well, with *Pisces III* busily at work on the sea bed for up to ten hours a day. Then came that fateful Wednesday.

It was while *Pisces III* was being hauled up after an uneventful but hard-working spell on the ocean bed that the mishap occurred. The hoist parted, and the mini-sub sank to the bottom again, where she lay helpless with her two-man crew trapped inside her.

A rescue operation was begun without a moment's delay. The *Vickers Voyager* sailed for the nearest big port, which was Cork, in southern Ireland, and at the same time Vickers Oceanics Ltd made arrangements for an earlier model of the submarine, *Pisces II*, to be flown to Cork from their works in the north of England. A more advanced version, *Pisces V*, was also despatched to the same destination, in this case from the other side of the Atlantic, aboard a Royal Canadian Airforce C130 transport aircraft.

Both these mini-subs reached Cork on the day after the accident and were loaded straight on board the *Vickers Voyager*. She sailed immediately back to the scene of the mishap, where the Royal Fleet Auxiliary vessel *Sir Tristram* was now standing by. Another Royal Navy ship, the survey vessel *Hecate*, had been called upon, and was due in the area very shortly. Both these ships carried special gear for recovering objects from great depths.

None of the experts involved in the rescue attempt underestimated its difficulties, the chief of which was that *Pisces III* was lying far too deep for divers to operate. The only way she could be salvaged – and, what was far more important, the lives of the two men inside saved – would be by attaching lifting gear to her by remote control.

In the minds of many of the rescuers was the grim recollection that only two months previously two men had died in similar circumstances in a mini-sub very like this one, at a depth of only a hundred metres. What was more, that accident had happened off the coast of Florida, in much clearer and calmer waters.

Visibility would pose great problems at the depth at which *Pisces III* lay. Very little daylight would penetrate so far. And the murky darkness of the ocean floor was not the only problem. Before the operation could even begin, the tiny vessel had to be found, and this was how the two Rogers came to be singing for their lives. . . .

To start with, all went well, even if time was rushing by. Sonar contact was established at 3 a.m. on the Friday, only two hours after the *Vickers Voyager*'s return from Cork.

Pisces V now went down to try to make visual contact. Her first dive brought no results, but a second from a more accurately plotted position was almost immediately successful. *Pisces V* was even able to attach a guideline to *Pisces III* before returning to the surface.

There was jubilation on board the rescue vessel. The great hurdle of locating the crippled sub had been surmounted. But there quickly came the sobering thought that there were only twenty-four hours left in which to accomplish the equally or even more difficult business of getting her up.

The next task was to attach a lifting cable to *Pisces III*. The first attempt was made by *Pisces II*, and it was now that things started to go wrong.

It wasn't *Pisces II*'s lucky day. She had already damaged the mechanical arm she would have to use in the rescue attempt. That had been repaired, but now, as she went down with the lifting cable, there were indications that she was leaking, and she had to return to the surface.

With that setback the situation suddenly began to look very grim. Time was really running out now. The last full day the two men could hope to survive in their underwater prison was rushing away. Not only that – the weather was bad and getting worse. And the rescuers themselves were becoming exhausted.

The deadline – the death-line – was only a few hours away. That sea-bed prison could soon become a tomb.

The rescue operation had become a really desperate race against time. The trapped men, who were in touch with the surface by telephone, reported that they were O.K. so far, but they and everyone else knew that the situation could change with terrifying suddenness. Within the extremely limited space of a vessel as small as *Pisces III*, the atmosphere could deteriorate within minutes to a deadly mixture of gases that would leave the occupants unconscious. All too soon after that they would die of carbon dioxide poisoning and oxygen starvation.

The chairman of Vickers Oceanics Ltd, Sir Leonard Redshaw, was under no illusion about the situation. To someone who asked how he saw the two men's chances, he replied, 'If they are to be brought up successfully, it is going to be a very, very narrow thing indeed.'

A gale warning was now in force in the area, and very heavy seas were running. In spite of this the rescue operation pressed ahead with the utmost speed. Relief workers were airlifted out to replace the now exhausted men on the *Vickers Voyager*, and buckled to the moment they got there.

It was now that the United States Navy lent a hand by flying in one of those bits of mechanical wizardry the Americans are so good at. This was a Controlled Underwater Recovery Vehicle, CURV for short – a highly technical underwater unmanned vessel operated by remote control.

Midnight came – and went. The rescue operation moved into the last day on which anything could possibly be done. It would have to be done, in fact, within the next hour or two, since *Pisces III*'s maximum period of endurance would be up in the small hours of the morning.

No more singing now, and very little other sign of life in the submarine, apart from a laconic word now and then. The two men in *Pisces III* had been told to restrict all forms of activity in order to eke out their remaining oxygen.

Dawn broke, grey and cold. The Atlantic was a wild waste of waters. The hours dragged slowly by.

At 9.15 there was reason to fear the worst. Voice contact with the two Rogers was lost. Increasingly urgent attempts were made to get through to them, but all came up against a blank wall of silence.

It was a frightening thing to have happened. Did it mean the trapped men had already sunk into a coma from which they would never wake? It seemed the only possible explanation. If either of them had still been conscious surely he would have replied?

Mercifully it was a false alarm. There were sighs of relief all round as communication was restored just as suddenly as it had been broken off. The break in contact had been caused by interference from instruments aboard the rescue vessels.

As a result of the scare, the rescuers intensified their efforts. They weren't going to be beaten now!

The breakthrough came when, very shortly after this heart-stopping incident, both *Pisces V* and CURV succeeded in attaching lifting cables to *Pisces III*. *Pisces V* then surfaced, while CURV, whose equipment included underwater television, stayed on the sea bed to monitor the lift-off.

Observers on the surface saw the most absorbing TV of their lives as they watched *Pisces III* stir, then rise slowly from what had so nearly been a watery grave.

It was 1.19 p.m. on Saturday, 1st September, 1973 when the mini-sub, hauled up slowly by the American vessel *John Cabot*, broke surface in heavy seas. She had been submerged for seventy-six hours – four hours longer than her estimated maximum endurance.

What happened after that was like the splash-down of a space capsule. A hatch opened, and one after the other the two 'jolly Rogers' climbed out, a little less jolly than usual, but none the worse for their hair-raising experience. They transferred from *Pisces III* to a waiting rubber dinghy which took them to the *Vickers Voyager*. From the *Voyager* a helicopter flew them to Cork, where they had a medical check-up and were pronounced surprisingly fit, considering that they had survived the deepest rescue in the history of the sea.

Man Overboard!

When Douglas Wardrop was two, he fell into a pond. Someone grabbed him and hauled him out just in time to save his life.

When he was three, he fell into another pond – one with lilies on it. This time he managed to get himself out.

When he was four he was living near the river Thames. One day he went fishing for tiddlers – and fell in. Again someone rescued him just in the nick of time.

When he was six and living by the sea, Douglas learned to swim. Under the circumstances, it wasn't a bad idea!

When he was fifteen, he joined the local Sea Cadets. On one weekend trip, the boat sank. Of course Douggie wasn't drowned. Nor, luckily, were any of the other cadets.

Douglas joined the merchant navy, and, when he was twenty-two, fell off the back of his ship in the middle of the Pacific Ocean. Or if it wasn't the middle, it might just as well have been. It was a 1500-kilometre swim to the nearest land.

At the time this happened, Douglas was second mate aboard a six-thousand-tonne freighter called the *British Monarch*. He ceased to be aboard very early in the morning of Sunday, 9th June, 1957, when the ship was four days out from Panama, bound for Japan.

For the better part of those four days the *Monarch* had been thumping her way across the largest and loneliest ocean in the world without even seeing another ship.

Douglas fell overboard just after 4 a.m., which wasn't the best time he could have chosen. At that hour of the morning the life of the ship was at its lowest ebb, and it was still dark. There was no one to hear or see him go.

Douglas had 'had the middle', as sailors put it. In other words he had been on duty for the middle watch, which lasts from midnight to 4 a.m. Those four hours had been uneventful, but towards the end of the watch he noticed that the log repeat in the chartroom wasn't working.

There are two kinds of ship's logs. One is a written record of her progress, giving details of course, speed, sea and wind conditions, and so on. The other is the mechanism which registers speed and distance travelled through the water – a sort of marine speedometer.

The *British Monarch*'s mechanical log was a very simple type, worked by a metal propeller-like spinner towed on a light line behind the ship. The spinner turns as it is drawn through the water, making the tow-line revolve, and this operates speed and distance dials on a clock-type instrument fixed on or near the stern rail of the vessel.

Many small craft such as cruising yachts carry this kind of log, and in their case the clock can be read directly without any trouble. With a ship of any size, however, it would be a nuisance to have to go right along to the stern, probably from the bridge, every time the log had to be read, so the information given by the log clock is relayed electrically to the navigating position, commonly called the chartroom.

It was this chartroom 'repeat' which Douglas had noticed was on the blink.

Douglas was the *Monarch*'s navigator, so it was his responsibility to see that the log was working properly. He suspected that the fault was in the relay – that was where trouble usually occurred – and that the clock itself was still working properly. This record of speed and distance run was only a rough and secondary method of navigation, so putting it right wasn't a matter of tremendous urgency. It could easily have waited till morning. But Douglas, who was a conscientious chap, decided to fix it straightaway.

When he came down from the bridge at the end of his watch, he made his way aft. The night was very dark and he had to use his torch.

The log clock was attached to a bracket extending about a metre from the stern rail. He climbed up on to the rail to examine it.

It was a silly and risky thing to do in the dark, especially with no one to keep an eye on him, and Douglas's only excuse was that he was so used to being at sea and had inspected the log so often before that he simply wasn't aware of the danger.

Shining his torch on the face of the log clock, he saw that it was registering correctly, which meant that, as he had thought, the fault was in the electrical relay to the chartroom. Probably, as usually happened, the contacts in the clock had become affected by damp or salt, or both. Steadying himself with the hand holding the torch, he began to unscrew the clock face.

It was then that it happened. There was nothing but darkness astern of the ship, and it is very difficult to keep one's balance when there is no visual point of reference for the eye to steady on. The ship was also rolling slowly, and Douglas, encumbered by the torch, had no real hand-hold. Suddenly he felt himself falling. . . .

It was eight metres from the ship's rail to the sea. He fell sprawling into the turbulence of the *Monarch*'s wake, and surfaced, gasping.

It had happened so quickly, but he kept his wits about him. The log line! It was his one chance of staying with the ship. It was trailing out there astern somewhere – over thirty metres of it.

He looked up, and there it was – a thin black thread against the sky. He hurled himself up and by a miracle was able to grab hold of it.

But he realised immediately that it wasn't going to work. The *Monarch* was steaming at ten knots, or about twenty kilometres an hour. This may not be very fast for a ship, but is a tremendous speed at which to be dragged through the water, especially the churning water of a ship's wake. Douglas was instantly subjected to a buffeting so violent that he could scarcely draw breath to shout, and when he did manage to do so, the seething sea filled his mouth. He could not keep his hold on the log line, and it burned his hands as it slipped through them. After only a few metres, he was forced to let go.

He was lucky (if you could call anyone in his situation lucky) that he hadn't become entangled in the line. If he had, he would quite certainly have been drowned.

When he had let go, all he could do was watch his ship steaming away into the darkness. He kept shouting, but he knew it wasn't any good. Even at her quietest a ship at sea makes a good deal of noise – more than enough to drown any puny human cry for help.

He had no hope of being either heard or seen. The men who had just come off watch would be thinking about getting into their bunks as soon as they could. Some of them might already be there, and fast asleep. And though there was a new watch on duty – including a new look-out on the bridge – their attention would be focussed on what lay ahead of the ship and not what she had left behind her.

The *British Monarch*'s towering stern grew smaller and less distinct until it merged into the pre-dawn darkness. The one or two lights Douglas could see aboard her grew fainter and fainter until they disappeared. The last to dwindle to a pin-point and vanish was her white stern light. After that Douglas was left, without sight or sign of mankind. He was utterly alone – one insignificant human being lost amid a vast and empty waste of waters.

While the ship was within sight, he had by instinct swum after her. Reason now told him that he was simply wasting his strength, and he stopped, treading water instead. It was a very hot night, and he had been wearing only a singlet and shorts when he fell overboard, so he wasn't encumbered with clothes, and found it easy enough to stay afloat. He wasn't likely to die of exposure either, as he might have done in northern waters.

But what good would that do beyond prolonging the agony for a few hours?

With an effort he pulled himself together and assessed the situation. What were his chances?

Straightaway he wrote off the chances of being picked up by any vessel except his own. Ships were so few and far between on that enormous expanse of ocean that the odds against that happening were not far short of astronomical.

No. The only hope he had would be if the *Monarch* turned back to look for him. But would she turn back?

Douglas tried to work it out. He knew that it all depended on the *Monarch*'s skipper. Captain Coutts was not only a warm and humane man, but a splendid navigator.

Turning back would cost time and money, but Douglas didn't think the *Monarch*'s captain would let that influence him. He would base his decision on whether he thought going back to look for his lost second mate would have any chance at all of being successful.

In a way, Douglas was lucky that he was a navigator himself. At least he had some idea what the chances of finding him were. Very, very slim, maybe, but not non-existent. Someone else, without his knowledge, might well have given up then and there, and that would have been the end. But Douglas knew it *could* be done, and he pinned his faith on Captain Coutts. The Old Man *would* turn back, if only because it was a challenge.

But, he realised, he was jumping the gun a bit. One thing was painfully obvious, and that was that no one, not even Captain Coutts, was going to find him for some while yet. So what he had got to do was hang on.

The daunting thought came to him that he could scarcely have chosen a worse time for his involuntary bathe, not only because he had fallen overboard in the darkest hour of the night, when the ship was at its most deserted, but also because the day now dawning was a Sunday. Sunday aboard the *Monarch*, as on board most ships, was lie-in day. Discipline and routine were relaxed, which meant it might easily be longer than it would have been on a weekday before he was missed.

The vast vault of the sky paled at last, then flushed in the east. Dawn broke. Douglas, still afloat and immeasurably grateful for daylight, whatever it might bring, was a pin-head on a pale blue ocean stretching emptily on all sides to the horizon. He turned and turned, searching that horizon, hoping against hope to see a ship. But there was no sign of one. Not even a wisp of funnel smoke. Nothing.

With daylight came company – some welcome and some not. A flock of small brown birds found him and flew around him curiously, one or two of them even dive-bombing him. He was glad to see the birds, but this life in the sky made him think of life in the sea, in particular of sharks. He put his face down into the water so that he could see below him – and there one was, circling ominously below him. How long had it been there? Was it circling to attack him? He kicked out hard, and the creature whisked away.

The sun climbed higher, burning down on his salt-drenched, unprotected head. His face and shoulders were getting sore with sun and salt, and his discomfort was greatly added to when he suddenly found himself in the midst of a shoal of electric eels, which stung him time and time again before they moved on.

Then came the prehistoric monster. It was in fact a giant turtle, though Douglas was none too clear about that at the time. Apparently it liked company too, and swam around him, snorting.

As the sun climbed higher and beat down more and more fiercely, Douglas began to feel light-headed. It was difficult to tell what was real and what was not. His strength was also beginning to fail. Afterwards he seemed to remember hanging on to the turtle for support, and it could have been that which saved his life.

He kept trying to work out how long it would be before the ship came back. *If* it came back. Of course it would – it must, it must!

How long it would take would depend on how long it was before he was missed, and that length of time would have to be doubled to take in the return journey.

If they missed him when the watch was changed at 8 a.m., that would be four hours after he'd fallen in. If at 9 a.m., it would be five. Twice four was eight, and twice five was ten. If it was eight, they would be back at about noon. If it was five, it would be two hours after that. *If* they came back. And if they found him if they *did* come back . . .

What, meanwhile, was happening aboard the *British Monarch*? Sunday had dawned with no interruption of normal routine. The morning watch had ended at 8 a.m. without any alarm being raised. The steward who took Douglas his morning tea found his cabin empty, but didn't attach any significance to it. He could have gone to the lavatory or the bathroom, or up on deck for a breather. It was hot below.

The first to miss Douglas was his best friend on board, the *Monarch*'s radio officer, Stan McNally. When Douglas didn't appear at breakfast, Stan, like the steward with the morning tea, thought nothing of it, at any rate at first. It was Sunday, and Douglas wasn't on watch until noon. He could easily be having a lie-in.

But something was bothering Stan, though he couldn't have said what. He went looking for his friend, and, when he couldn't find him, told the captain.

Captain Coutts immediately ordered a search of the ship. It was a very thorough search, but the second mate was nowhere to be found.

The inference was obvious. He must have gone over the side. He couldn't have thrown himself over, because Douglas Wardrop simply wasn't that type. It could only have been an accident.

Captain Coutts had a decision to make: whether to turn back or not. It would cost time and money if he did, but he didn't hesitate. If there was the slightest chance of the man being found alive, he'd got to take it. He'd have done the same for any member of his crew, however humble, because that was the sort of man he was.

It was now 8.30 a.m., or about four and a half hours since the second mate had last been seen. Captain Coutts decided to run back for an equivalent period of time. It was going to be a very long shot indeed, but there was just a chance.

The captain turned the *British Monarch* round and headed her carefully back the way she had come, making due allowance for an ocean current which had been setting the ship slightly to the southward of her compass course. The helmsman didn't need to be told to steer with extra care.

An hour passed. Two. Three. Four. Visibility was good, but to those on the *British Monarch* that was a mixed blessing. The vast plain of the ocean the ship was ploughing through had never looked emptier. . . .

When Douglas first spotted the ship, he couldn't believe his eyes. It was the *Monarch*, there could be no doubt of that. 'They *have* come back!' he kept telling himself. 'I knew they would!' At the same time it seemed too incredible to be true. The ship wasn't really there at all. She must be a mirage – an illusion – something he could see only because he wanted to see it so much. By this time he was quite light-headed.

He shut his eyes and opened them again, expecting the ship to have disappeared. It hadn't. On the contrary, it was getting bigger. It looked like the *Monarch*. It *was* the *Monarch*! His excitement gave way to anxiety. The ship's masts weren't quite in line, which

meant she wasn't heading directly for him. On her present course she would pass some distance – perhaps five hundred metres – away. How terrible, for her to be so near and yet so far! Suppose she didn't find him now? But if she didn't come straight to him, what chance was there of anyone aboard her spotting him – a mere speck on the surface of that sun-dazzled ocean?

Mac. He put all his faith in Mac Taylor. Mac, the *British Monarch*'s third mate, had the sharpest eyes in the ship. Mac would spot him!

Meanwhile, at the same time that these urgent hopes and fears were torturing his second mate, Captain Coutts was beginning to think his turning back had been in vain. He had run the full distance to the estimated position where the mishap must have occurred, and had seen nothing. He felt he'd been foolish ever to have thought he might.

It was nearly half past one. He decided to make a circular sweep until the half hour, then resume his course for Japan.

Douglas saw the gap between the *Monarch*'s masts widen. She was turning away! She had come so close, but now she was altering course and leaving him to his fate!

The little time that remained ticked away. The *British Monarch* continued her sweep, a lot less hopefully now. It was merely a matter of conscientiously following out what she had set herself to do.

But, just as conscientiously, every member of her crew who could be spared from other essential duties still searched the sea from her decks and superstructure.

Among them was the third mate, Mac Taylor. And it was he who, at almost the last moment, triumphantly justified Douglas's faith in him. At 1.27 p.m., with only three minutes more to go, Mac swept the ocean yet again with his binoculars, and steadied them on a tiny object in the water.

The object was waving. Within minutes, Douglas was safe back aboard the *British Monarch*.

Perhaps Douglas's mother may be allowed the last word. She of course didn't know anything about her son's latest adventure until it was all over, and would have been worried stiff if she had.

As it was, remembering those previous escapades of Douglas's, all she said was, 'I'm not surprised. I always knew he was water-proof.'

The Ice Sailors

The floe was enormous and so thick that multi-engined aircraft could land on it. The four men who had been flown in and who had now pitched their tents upon it weren't in the least worried about the firmness of the foundation of their little encampment. They were to change their minds dramatically before their ordeal on the ice floe was over.

The four men were Russians: Ivan Papanin, Ernst Krenkel, Peter Shirshov and Eugene Federov. They were meteorologists, and Papanin was their leader. They were landed on the floe on 21st May, 1937, with the idea of living there for the next few months to study conditions in the Arctic.

Once the aircraft which had landed them had taken off again, they were oppressed by a feeling of overwhelming loneliness and desolation. How, they wondered, could anyone live in such a totally inhospitable world? They had a strange foreboding that they would never see their homes again. Nor were they far wrong. But, as Papanin briskly reminded the others, they had come there of their own free will, and for a very definite purpose. They had a job of work to do.

And so they proceeded to settle in. They pitched three tents in the middle of the floe – one to serve as their living quarters, one for stores, and a third to do duty as a radio 'shack'.

They soon established a routine, taking weather observations daily and keeping in radio touch with Moscow via the Russian icebreaker *Murmanets*, which served as a relay station.

It was a tough but monotonous life, enlivened only by occasional visits from polar bears. Merely surviving in such bitter conditions was pretty well a full-time job, but the four men gradually got used to it.

The floe drifted south, swept by savage snowstorms for much of the time. At one point it looked as though it might break up on a dangerous reef off the coast of Greenland, but it survived that hazard.

The four meteorologists continued to carry out their scientific duties as regularly and conscientiously as ever, and by February 1938 – some eight months after they had landed on the floe – they felt that they had gathered enough data for the expedition to have proved worthwhile.

By this time the floe had drifted into warmer – or at least less cold – waters. Life was a little easier than it had been, and they could be excused for thinking that the toughest part of the job was over.

As it turned out, it was now that their troubles really started. One of their biggest problems so far had been boredom. Their meteorological duties occupied only a fraction of their time, and the weather didn't encourage them to stay out in the open any longer than they had to. At the same time their living quarters were extremely cramped and uncomfortable. There wasn't much they could do there during the day except read or write or, perhaps, play chess. This is what Ivan Papanin and Ernst Krenkel were doing on the day they and their companions got the shock of their lives.

The weather at the time was 'normal'. In other words, a blizzard was raging. Actually, they'd had the same sort of thing for the past six days, during which time they'd been drifting blind, the storm never clearing enough for them to be able to use their sextant and fix their position. But it didn't matter. It was only a case of waiting until the clouds cleared away, or so they thought . . .

Papanin and Krenkel were in the middle of a game when there came a deafening report, like the firing of a big gun very close at hand. All four men started. The chessmen shook on the board.

'What was that?' Krenkel asked.

'The ice,' Papanin said. 'We'd better go and see.'

As he finished speaking, another loud report sounded, followed this time by a gigantic rending noise. All four men got outside the tent as fast as they could to find out what was going on.

As Papanin had said, it was the ice. The floe had split only a few metres from the tent.

Even as they stared at the fissure, there was a third loud crack and it lengthened like a sudden, jagged dart of lightning, shooting along close past the igloo they had built out of ice blocks to house their stores, on the near side.

The two sides of the fissure were grinding together as the ice heaved under their feet. What if the crevasse became so wide that they could not cross it? Their living tent was on one side of it, and the storehouse on the other.

'The stores!' Pananin cried. 'We must save the stores!'

For the next few hours the four men worked frantically to move first the stores and then everything else to the centre of the floe, which they thought would be the safest place, though they couldn't even be sure of that. From time to time there were further loud reports, sometimes singly and sometimes in fusillades, like bursts of machine-gun fire. The ice kept trembling and shaking, sometimes violently, as though the whole floe was about to disintegrate. At that stage Papanin and his comrades were convinced their last hour had come.

They did the only thing they could do, which was to establish a new camp at the centre of the floe. They covered their heaped-up stores with sheeting and re-erected their tents.

That night they lay huddled in the living tent, listening to the noise made by the ice breaking up all around them, and expecting to be thrown at any moment into the freezing sea. But their new base escaped destruction. How lucky they had been became apparent next day, when they saw nothing but broken ice in all directions. The whole huge ice field had split up into fragments.

Things now took a slight turn for the better. The sky cleared and they were able to use the sextant. Fixing their position, they discovered that they had been drifting in a south-westerly direction at roughly thirty kilometres per day.

Now that they knew at least roughly where they were, they no longer felt so cut off from the rest of the world, especially as they were able to report their position to the *Murmanets*. Their spirits rose still further when they received a radiogram from Moscow telling them that the *Murmanets* and two other ice-breakers were steaming to their rescue.

But their ordeal was by no means over. The weather worsened again, the wind rising and the temperature dropping as another blizzard came shrieking in. The four men were soaking wet and half frozen, and their now frighteningly small floe was rocking like a boat.

They had very little hope left now. They knew only too well that the further the ice drifted to the southward, the more rapidly it would disintegrate. They were sure their days, if not their hours, were numbered.

On 6th February they could both see and hear evidence that what they feared had begun to happen. There was a constant, thunderous booming as the floes crashed together, and a gigantic groaning and scraping as they rode up over one another. The four scientists knew that at any moment one of the nearest of those great slabs of ice could come riding relentlessly over their own precarious refuge.

The final blow came with a radio message from the *Murmanets* to the effect that she was ice-bound. There was no word at all from the other two ice-breakers, and the marooned men could only assume that they were in the same situation. It really did look like the end.

On 8th February the wind rose to new heights of fury, screaming across that world of frozen chaos with such speed and strength that it threatened to blow the tents away. The four men rescued the radio equipment just in the nick of time before the tent which housed it was ripped from its moorings and disappeared into the storm. The living tent was ballooning out and threatening to follow it at any moment, so they desperately set to and built a snow hut into which they crawled, to lie there exhausted in their sodden clothes.

They were convinced that this was the end – that they must either freeze to death there on the floe, or drown when it finally disintegrated.

But again they were wrong. They somehow managed to survive for a whole week in their snow hut, and then at last rescue came. They were sighted by the two icebreakers they had been unable to contact. One of the vessels took them on board, desperately in need of warmth and nourishment, but otherwise very little the worse for their ordeal.

Soon afterwards they were back in Moscow, where they were accorded a heroes' welcome which they thoroughly deserved. Their nine-months' drift on the ice floe, in the course of which they had gathered a great deal of valuable data, must be ranked as one of the greatest of all feats of Arctic exploration.

The Light on the Rock

The men aboard the fishing boat strained their eyes through the darkness. Out to seaward there was a glow of light which grew in intensity even as they stared at it.

One of them said, 'The Eddystone's bright tonight.'

Another said, 'It isn't the light. The lighthouse is on fire!'

The lighthouse they were referring to was the second to be built on the Eddystone Rocks, the deadly dangerous triple reef which lies some 23 kilometres south-west of Plymouth. At low tide a stretch of roughly 180 metres of this reef is exposed, but the whole jagged expanse is invisible at high tide, and of course at any state of the tide in thick darkness and bad weather.

The Eddystone rocks have been a threat to the prosperity of Plymouth ever since that place became a port, since most of the vessels using it had to pass uncomfortably close to them. As early as 1664 the people of Plymouth presented a petition for a lighthouse on the Eddystone to Trinity House, that ancient and splendid organisation which has for centuries been responsible for the construction, positioning and maintenance of lighthouses, lightships and buoys around the coasts of the British Isles.

For what were perfectly good reasons at the time, Trinity House turned down this petition. Thirty years later, during the reign of William and Mary, a patent was granted for the erection of a lighthouse on the reef, the cost to be defrayed by levying dues on vessels using the port.

The way was now clear for an Eddystone lighthouse. So far, no one had ever built a lighthouse on a rock, for the simple reason that doing so presented the most enormous and daunting problems.

The difficulties were even more formidable in the case of the Eddystone than they might have been elsewhere, because of the reef's position and local weather conditions. The rocks were exposed to the full force of the prevailing westerlies sweeping in from the Atlantic, as well as to the strong tides and currents which scoured through the comparatively narrow limits of the English Channel. Even on calm days there could be rough water breaking on those jagged rocks, or at least too much of a swell for a boat to make a landing.

The lighthouse was to be built of stone, which meant a very large number of heavy blocks would have to be brought out from Plymouth aboard small boats. And often, having brought them out, they might have to be taken back again, since landing them on the reef would be possible only for an hour or so either side of low tide, and in the calmest of weather. Much would depend, in those days before boats had engines, on the strength and direction of the wind.

Merely getting the necessary building material to the site would therefore be a formidable task in itself.

The building of the lighthouse was undertaken by a very odd character named Henry Winstanley. Winstanley's talents and enthusiasms included designing, inventing, painting pictures and playing practical jokes. He was also quite a good conjurer.

Henry Winstanley's lighthouse was no joke. It was the biggest challenge of his life, and one he met with considerable success, even if the result didn't last very long. His lighthouse took four years to build, and, as was usually the case with anything Winstanley undertook, a number of strange things happened during that time, including his being taken prisoner by a French privateer. Fortunately the King of France quickly ordered his release.

At last, at the end of those four years, Henry Winstanley was able to light the giant candles in the lantern of his lighthouse. That night, which was the night of 14th November, 1698, the lighting-up of the lighthouse was witnessed by crowds of spectators along the coast and hundreds of others in a whole fleet of small boats.

The lighthouse was put severely to the test that first winter. At one point bad weather marooned Winstanley and his men there for five long weeks. But lessons were learned, and profited by. During the following year the diameter of the lighthouse tower was increased from 4.87 to 7.31 metres, and its overall height to 36.57 metres.

The greatest tribute that can be paid to Henry Winstanley is the fact that, while his lighthouse stood sentinel there, not a single ship was lost on the Eddystone, whereas previously wrecks on the killer reef had been tragically frequent.

The lighthouse survived a fourth winter, but on the night of 26th November, 1703, came the greatest storm within living memory. Huge seas and winds of hurricane force caused many casualties in the English Channel that night, including the light on the Eddystone.

Just what happened, no one ever knew, because no one survived to tell the tale. People on shore maintained that there was a light in the lantern as usual just before midnight, but when dawn broke there was nothing except debris to show that a lighthouse had ever stood on the reef.

Winstanley was in the lighthouse at the time, and he died as he had lived – dramatically. The value of his contribution to safety at sea was proved just as dramatically, and almost immediately, when, only two nights later, a big British merchantman homeward bound from Virginia with a cargo of tobacco was wrecked on the Eddystone. Two of her crew managed to get away in one of the ship's boats, but the rest died.

So Winstanley's brave venture ended in ruin. But the need for a lighthouse on the Eddystone had been amply demonstrated, and it was not long before plans were laid for building another.

Again, as in Winstanley's case, an unlikely person was given the job. His name was John Rudyerd, and he was a silk merchant, which is surely about as far as you can get from blocks of granite. But Rudyerd, like Winstanley, was a man of many ideas, and showed a good deal of ingenuity in carrying them out.

The lighthouse Rudyerd visualised was in fact entirely different from Winstanley's. He never seriously thought of using granite blocks at all. This was the great age of wooden ships, the 'hearts of oak', and what Rudyerd planned was a structure not of stone but of wood braced with iron. It would be slender and tapering, rather like a ship's mast. It would also have the same cross-section as a ship's mast. It would have none of the flat surfaces which Winstanley's tower had had, but would be round and smooth so that it would deflect the force of both wind and waves. It would even 'give' a little in storm conditions.

This second Eddystone lighthouse was transferred from paper to practical reality by the Master Shipwrights of Her Majesty Queen Anne's Dockyard at Woolwich, who proved that they were indeed masters of their trade. In due course a new tower, 21.33 metres high, was erected on the Eddystone. Once again a light beamed out to warn vessels away from those treacherous rocks.

Rudyerd's lighthouse survived much longer than Winstanley's – for forty-six years, to be precise. And the eventual destruction of this tower, which had been built by shipwrights like the mast of a ship, was, ironically, caused by that other great hazard to ships at sea – fire!

It was blowing hard, that last night, and the tower was creaking and groaning loudly. You could even feel it sway. But none of those things caused any worry. It had been behaving like that in rough weather for the best part of half a century.

Henry Hall, the oldest of the three lighthouse keepers, went on duty at midnight. Henry was, incredibly, ninety-four years old, but still active, still spry. He went through his routine checks, then settled down. As would have been the case if he had been aboard ship, his watch was due to end at 4 a.m.

It was about two o'clock, roughly halfway through his watch, when thick, choking black smoke came pouring down from the top of the lighthouse. It had an acrid smell of the tallow from which the candles were made. The lantern was on fire!

Henry shouted an alarm, then rushed down to rouse his companions, which took some time, for they were sound asleep a long way below him. Then all three of them seized leather buckets and rushed up to fight the fire.

It was hopeless. The flames had got much too firm a hold. Roaring to the bellows of the strong wind, they turned the lighthouse into a great flaring torch.

Then a particularly dreadful thing happened. The lead sheeting protecting the top of the lighthouse melted, and a shower of molten

metal came raining down. As old Henry Hall stood gaping up at what was happening, a gobbet of fiery, liquid lead fell right into his mouth. The only thing he could do was to swallow it, and he was in agony from then on.

The three men fought desperately to check the fire, but the fire made a mockery of their puny efforts. It burned steadily down the tower until it seemed the keepers must be consumed by it too. They would be roasted alive. They dared not leave the lighthouse because of the hail of burning timbers and molten metal that was hurtling down outside, and there was no refuge on the reef. There was a cave-like cleft in the rocks on the north-east side where they might find shelter later, but at present, at that state of the tide, it was under water.

Then the situation improved a little. When it reached the lower, sea-drenched timbers of the lighthouse, the fire's worst fury was checked. And the tide was falling, however slowly. At last the three men nerved themselves and made a dash for the fissure in the rocks. It was still being scoured by surging seas, but there were mooring rings there to which they could cling to stop themselves being swept away.

They managed to hang on there, battered and half drowned, until at last the tide had ebbed enough to be no longer a danger. After that they crouched, shivering, on the reef, waiting and hoping numbly for rescue.

It was 10 a.m. when, at last, a fishing boat arrived. The weather was far too bad for the boat to attempt a landing, so instead it anchored on the weather side as close in as its skipper dared, and drifted a small boat in on the end of a rope. The men in the boat threw a line to the castaway keepers on the reef and dragged them one by one out through the surf. As soon as they were all in the small boat, it was hauled back to the larger vessel.

Thus were the lives of the three lighthouse keepers saved. One of them, the youngest, suffered no real physical or other harm, but the ordeal the other two had been through had been more than they could bear. The second youngest came out of it so mentally disturbed that he disappeared very shortly after being brought ashore and was never seen in that part of the world again. As for poor old Henry Hall, he died twelve days after the fire. An autopsy revealed a piece of lead nearly ten centimetres across in his stomach.

With the destruction of Rudyerd's lighthouse, the Eddystone rocks again became as great a danger to shipping as they had ever been. Two brave failures to establish a permanent light on the reef had proved how difficult the task was, but no one with any sense and knowledge of the sea was in two minds about the need to try again, and as soon as possible. Third time lucky, maybe?

The luck, if it can be called that, lay in there being just the right man on hand for the job. He was John Smeaton, a brilliant young scientist and technician who had been elected a Fellow of the learned Royal Society when he was still under thirty years of age, and who had recently earned himself a great reputation as an engineer.

When John Smeaton took on the task of building the third Eddystone lighthouse, he went into the whole thing very carefully indeed, and came to a number of definite and important conclusions about both design and materials. He favoured a strong and very heavy all-stone tower, which would oppose the sea with its sheer weight as well as its strength. He also wanted a much bigger base, which was where the sea struck hardest, with a comparatively slender tower above it. Finally, he planned to dovetail the great stone blocks, so that none of them could be shifted separately. His object in this respect was to produce as nearly as possible the equivalent of an edifice in solid stone.

John Smeaton's lighthouse took just over three years to build. When it was finished, there was again a very welcome light on the Eddystone. But again, as in the past, there were people who predicted that this lighthouse would sooner or later suffer the fate of its predecessors, probably in some storm or other. However, three years after it was completed, it remained standing after a tremendous gale which wrought havoc in the English Channel. After this, the general feeling, particularly in the Plymouth area, was that if it could survive such a storm, it would survive anything.

The prediction was proved valid. Smeaton's formidable stone

tower stood bravely on the Eddystone rocks, beaming out its life-saving light over the sea, for well in excess of a hundred years. And when a weakness did develop, it was not in the lighthouse but in the rock on which it stood. The action of the sea and the weight of the lighthouse – nearly 1000 tonnes of stone – combined to undermine the foundations. As a result the lighthouse had developed a 'shake', which was slowly but none the less surely getting worse.

In the year 1877, Trinity House's Engineer-in-Chief, James Douglass, announced that he was to supervise the building of a fourth tower on the Eddystone.

This new lighthouse turned out to be the finest of them all. Built (thanks to the coming of the marine engine and advances in building techniques) in under four years, Douglass's tower is twice as tall as Smeaton's, the centre of its lantern being forty-one metres above high water level, compared with Smeaton's twenty-two metres.

Smeaton's lighthouse had stood there in lonely bravery so long, defying the worst that the wind and the waves could do, that people hated to see it go. But then someone had a bright idea, and the upper part was dismantled and re-erected on Plymouth Hoe, where it still stands. The stump was left on the reef, 36 metres from Douglass's tower, which today still beams out its warnings to shipping.

Winstanley ... Rudyerd ... Smeaton ... Douglass; but remember also all those successive crews of lighthouse keepers, and the men ferrying reliefs and supplies out to those dangerous rocks. They were all men who liked to do something unusual, preferably with a spice of danger in it.

Through their efforts, and at the risk of – sometimes the cost of – their lives, many, many souls have been saved from the sea.

Dive to Danger

The men on the bridge of the U.S. Coastguard destroyer *Paulding* stared in horror as the submarine S.4 surfaced right in front of their bows. The destroyer was steaming at eighteen knots, and the submarine was so close that it was impossible for her to slow down or turn away.

A minute or so later the inevitable collision occurred. The *Paulding* rammed the S.4 abreast of her conning tower with such force that the impact lifted the destroyer's bows right out of the water.

The submarine disappeared beneath the surface. Oil came welling up from her, but nothing else. None of her crew surfaced, alive or dead, so there was at least hope that she had not been too badly damaged.

Both vessels were American, and the collision had taken place in inshore American waters, off the small New England port of Provincetown. The two ships were taking part in a naval exercise at the time.

Immediately the incident occurred, the *Paulding* lowered a lifeboat and positioned a marker buoy, but her own damage was so serious that that was all she could do. With a six-metre gash on her port side forward she headed for the nearest beach to run herself aground.

Meanwhile an intensive rescue operation had been set in motion. Ships from a dozen of America's Atlantic ports hurried to the scene, while four U.S. Navy divers rushed by road to Provincetown from the neighbouring harbour of Newport.

One of these four was Chief Diver Thomas Eadie, who had had considerable experience of working on sunken submarines, and who was considered to be one of the best underwater men the U.S. Navy had. He was to prove that beyond the shadow of a doubt before this emergency was over.

The S.4 had a crew of forty men. She had gone down in roughly thirty metres of water, which was a reasonable depth for divers to work at, provided conditions were reasonable. Unfortunately the incident had occurred during the winter – on 17th December, 1927 – and the weather was bad, with strong winds and rough seas.

Nothing daunted, Tom Eadie went down as soon as he had arrived and had got suited up. He found the S.4 without too much trouble, and reported her condition to the surface by telephone. He said her hull was smashed in amidships, and her control room wrecked. Then came the great news.

'There are men alive in the torpedo compartment.'

'How many?' the rescuers asked anxiously.

'Six.'

Eadie had been talking in code with the men in the S.4 by hammering on the steel hull with a heavy wrench. Laboriously they hammered back, telling those on the surface to hurry. They said the air in their confined space was bad and getting worse.

Contact with the imprisoned men must have raised their spirits enormously, but Eadie's own situation was perilous. The submarine was a mass of tangled wreckage which confronted him with hazards literally at every turn, and he had to battle against strong currents and swirling mud.

A sudden jerk brought him up short. His helmet had fouled the S.4's twisted radio aerial. He managed to free himself, and when he reported that he had done so, was ordered up to the surface.

It was now the turn of diver 'Mike' Michaels to go down, in even worse conditions. The weather had deteriorated a lot. A full gale was blowing, and the temperature had dropped to near-freezing. Waves up to three metres high were surging across the diving area, which meant a constant variation in water pressure on the man below. The sea exerted an enormous pressure on the diver, causing intense pain, especially in the ears. It could burst a man's eardrums, and even kill.

Conditions on the sea bed were next to impossible, and before long the same thing happened to Michaels as had happened to Eadie. He became entangled in the wreckage of the submarine. He

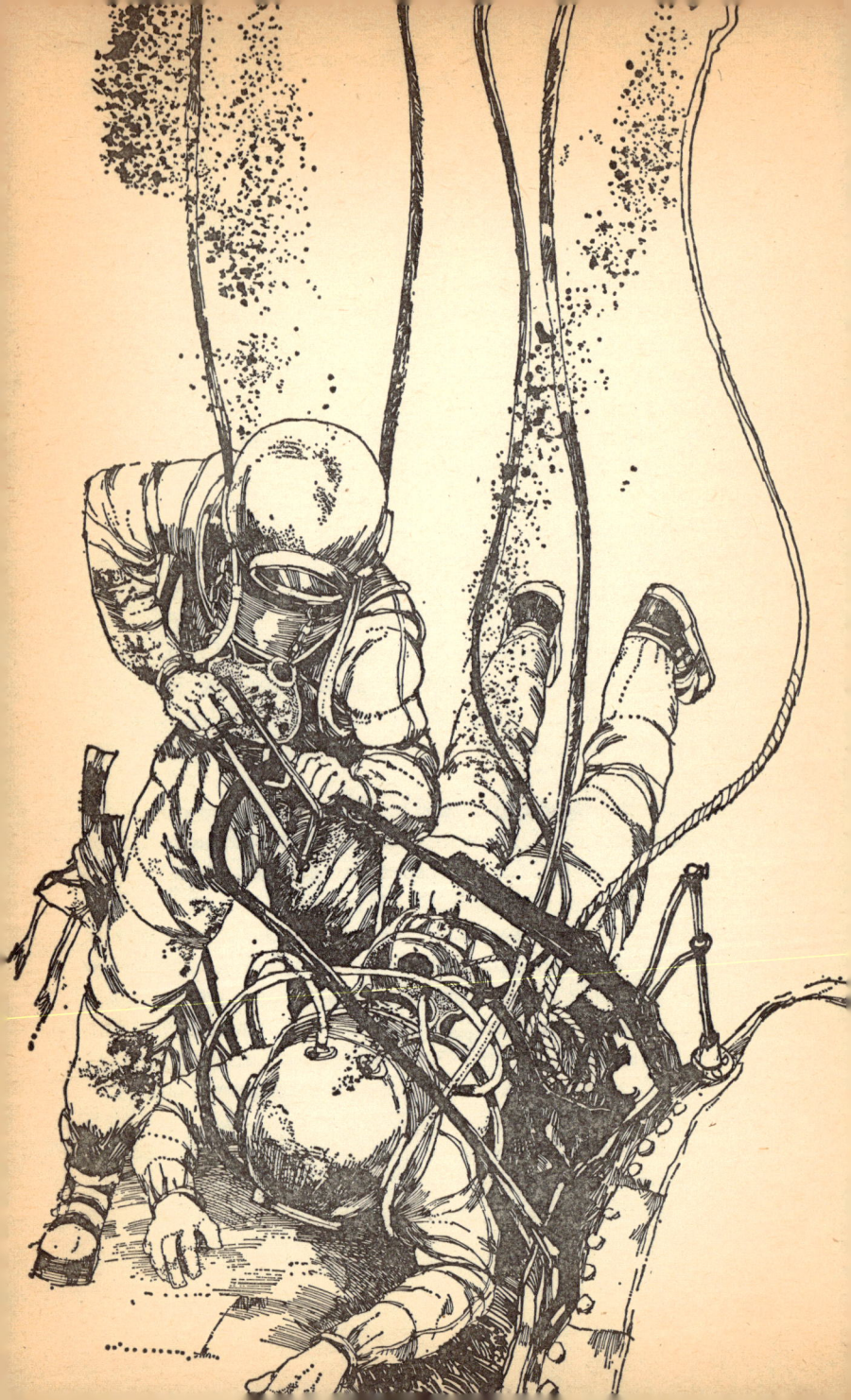

found himself in a far worse plight than Eadie, however, because he couldn't free himself.

The first the men on the surface knew of the drama below was when, after a period of silence, Michaels' voice sounded hoarsely up over his telephone line.

'I'm caught,' Michaels said. 'Send down cutters. I've got to have cutters.' And then, sharply, 'Send Eadie.'

When a diver surfaces, he has to spend a period of time in a decompression chamber, where the pressure he has been subjected to can be gradually adjusted to normal. Otherwise he may suffer the agonising and sometimes fatal condition known as 'the bends'. After that, in most cases – and certainly in the case of a dive as exhausting as the one Eadie had just completed – he needs to have several hours' rest before going down again.

Eadie was still in the decompression chamber when Michaels' call for help came through. He shouldn't have dived again for quite some time, but he took no heed of that. Michaels was not only a colleague he respected for his skill and courage, but a friend. Within minutes of hearing the news he was getting suited up again, as fast as he could.

The weather was worse than ever now, and the temperature still lower. But time was vital. It was a matter of life and death not only for the men in the submarine but also for the trapped diver. In fact his release was a priority because he was in more immediate danger than they were, and also because his release could be an important factor in their rescue.

To save precious minutes, Eadie put on only one of his usual three woollen undersuits. Also, because he couldn't use the cutters if he was wearing gloves, he had to go down with his hands bare.

To be sure of finding Michaels without delay, he went down the latter's line, taking with him, in addition to the wire-cutters, a hammer and chisel, a small crowbar, and a 1000-watt lamp.

Michaels was lying face-down in the wreckage, with his heavy airhose and lifeline in a hopeless tangle on top of him. Loops of both hose and line were caught up in the debris on either side.

Peering through the thick, swirling water with the aid of his powerful lamp, Eadie discovered that the main cause of the trouble was a U-shaped steel bar. He realised that to release Michaels he would have to cut through the bar, and that the wire-cutters he'd brought down with him, powerful though they were, were no use for that. What he needed was a hacksaw.

He telephoned his request to the surface, and a hacksaw was sent down his lifeline, attached to a heavy shackle to speed its descent. With the saw in his already numbed hands, Eadie turned to start the job.

It was then he discovered that something was gravely wrong with Mike Michaels. His diving suit was cut and water had got into it. He had lost consciousness, and only the pressure of air in his helmet was keeping him alive, but for how long?

The temptation to speed up the job of sawing through the steel bar was tremendous, but Eadie resisted it. He had to go carefully in case the hacksaw blade broke. Getting another one sent down to him would mean a delay that would almost certainly be fatal.

The sawing took nearly an hour, and by the end of that time Eadie had himself sunk into a sort of coma. He moved the hacksaw back and forth, back and forth, more like an automaton than a human being. His own suit had torn and filled with water up to neck level.

At last it was done. The bar was severed.

As it parted, an eerie thing happened. Mike Michaels' suited body, now buoyant, floated up and away, disappearing from Eadie's sight in the streaming mud. It was almost as though he had deserted the man who had come to rescue him.

Eadie signalled that Michaels was free, and that he himself was just about at the end of his tether. He was hauled up without the usual stop on the way, and rushed to the decompression chamber. The first thing he did when his helmet was unscrewed was to ask how Mike was.

Michaels was already in the decompression chamber. He had been picked up, floating, stiff as a board. Eadie joined his fellow diver in the decompression chamber and, still in his sodden woollen undersuit, cut away Michaels' gloves, diving dress and undergarments, then wrapped him in blankets soaked in hot water. Only then did he strip off and seek the same grateful warmth himself.

The two divers were in the decompression chamber for three hours, at the end of which Michaels was still in a bad way. A U.S. Navy destroyer rushed him to the naval hospital in Boston, Massachusetts, where he made a slow recovery.

Like all too many submarine rescue attempts, the great efforts made to save the lives of the men entombed in the S.4 were doomed to failure. Their signals grew fainter and fainter, and finally ceased. Endless difficulties of one kind and another, the weather prominent among them, meant that it was the following spring before the submarine was raised.

But one life was saved from the sea. Thanks to Chief Diver Tom Eadie, Mike Michaels lived to continue his brave and useful life in one of the most hazardous of all professions.

Tom Eadie's bravery was without parallel in the history of the United States Navy. His country recognised that by awarding him the Congressional Medal of Honor – the equivalent of the British V.C.

A Girl called Grace

The Longstone lighthouse was a family business. In that tall 'house' on a rock lived lighthouse-keeper William Darling with his wife and children. While he maintained the light, his wife looked after the family, and they all did their share of the odd jobs that have to be done if you live in such a home. The Darling lighthouse was a happy place.

In due course the younger Darling children left home, but the oldest, a girl called Grace, stayed on with her parents on their wind- and wave-swept rock. It was Grace, a frail, delicate girl, who was destined to become Britain's greatest heroine in the history of the sea.

Grace's day of destiny – and that of nine other people – was 6th September, 1838. It was a day of storms.

The Longstone is the furthest to seaward of the Farne Islands, which lie off the coast of Northumberland. The islands are a menace to coastal vessels, especially when bad weather comes in from the north or east, threatening to drive them on to the land.

The paddle steamer *Forfarshire*, owned by the Dundee and Hull Steam Packet Company, had to face this hazard one stormy night in September, 1838.

The *Forfarshire*, an almost new vessel, was on her regular run from Hull to Dundee. She had a crew of twenty-two and a number of passengers on board. She was also carrying a mixed cargo of ironmongery, textiles, machinery and other miscellaneous items.

As the *Forfarshire* thrashed her way up the east coast of England, the weather got steadily worse. The nor'-nor'-east wind increased in strength, and was accompanied by heavy rain squalls. The ship was rolling and plunging, throwing up great clouds of spray. Several of the passengers were seasick.

The captain was suffering in a different way. He was worried. He

44

was a man of considerable experience in the coastal trade, but he wasn't sure of his ship. She had developed leaks in two of her boilers only a few hours out from Hull, and this had severely reduced the power obtainable from her engines.

The chief engineer was worried too. In his view, as he said to the captain, it was always better to be safe than sorry. He advised turning back, but the captain overrode him. After all, he had a fine ship, hadn't he? And a fine reputation to maintain. He wasn't going to turn tail just because the wind was blowing a bit harder than it usually did.

The captain demanded increased pressure in the remaining boilers, and the sweating men below decks did their best to give him what he wanted. But it was an impossible task. The boiler room became overheated, with jets and clouds of steam everywhere. Many of the stokers were lucky to escape scalding.

The battle was in vain. One by one the remaining boiler fires went out, which meant the ship had lost almost all her power. She was at the mercy of the wind and sea.

The *Forfarshire* struggled on against a gale roaring in from starboard, which was the worst direction it could have blown from, since it was setting her on to the coast. She was making hardly any headway at all, and, to make matters worse, she had now sprung a leak. Those of her male passengers who were capable of it were called upon to help her crew man the pumps.

It was no use. In spite of heroic efforts on the pumps to keep her afloat, the water level was creeping up inside her. She sank lower and lower, with great seas breaking more and more frequently over her starboard rail. The hiss of steam escaping from her boilers grew louder and louder.

Late that evening, the *Forfarshire*'s paddles stopped turning. Her machinery had given up the ghost.

She now had only one hope left. The *Forfarshire* belonged to that transitional age when ships had sails as well as engines. The captain ordered her sails to be set.

By this time the captain was a very worried man indeed. In the forefront of his mind was the thought that the gale had blown him too far in towards the coast. Somehow he had to get round the Farne Islands, which lay directly in his path, and he didn't know how he was going to be able to do it.

Night fell. The north-easterly blew harder than ever. The *Forfarshire* staggered on through the gale-filled dark.

Suddenly there came a shout from one of the look-outs.

'Light ahead, sir! Fine on the starboard bow!'

'Very good,' the captain said.

A light was a blessing on a night like that, and no doubt the *Forfarshire*'s skipper was greatly relieved to see it. But it was now that he made a fatal mistake. There were two lighthouses on the Farnes, and for some reason he decided that the light he could see was the lighthouse on the Inner Farne, the island nearest the mainland. He therefore ordered an alteration of course to the westward which would take his ship – or so he believed – through the channel between the Farnes and the Northumberland coast.

Actually the light the look-out had spotted was the beam from the Darlings' lighthouse, the Longstone, on the eastern or seaward side of the Farnes.

Eased off the wind a little, the *Forfarshire* began to sail easier and faster. The only trouble was, she was now driving hard for Big Harcar, the murderous outcrop of rock which lay between the islands.

A little while later a great wave lifted her and threw her on to the reef with such force that many of her crew and passengers were thrown to the deck and several injured. Then rang out that most dreaded order of all: 'Abandon ship! Abandon ship!'

What followed was shameful. The ship's boat had been turned out on the starboard side, ready for lowering. The *Forfarshire*'s first and second mates, together with half a dozen other members of the crew, made straight for it and left the ship. They vanished into the seething darkness, never to be seen again. Loss of life at sea is a sad and tragic thing, but it is hard to feel sorry for these particular men.

The rest of the crew and the passengers could only cling desperately to anything they could find while the ship slammed down on the reef. Again . . . again . . . and again. The fourth time she did it, she broke in half, just aft of her paddle-wheels, and the forward part, with most of those left on board, was swept away into the howling night. Those remaining on the after part continued to hang on for dear life.

The captain had disappeared, and it was the *Forfarshire*'s third mate, a man of very different calibre from his brother officers, who now took charge. He yelled encouragement to everyone, urging them not to give up either their handholds or their hopes of being saved. They weren't finished yet!

There was truth in what he said. The tide was ebbing, and soon what remained of the *Forfarshire* would be high if not dry on the rocks. And though it might seem as though that terrible night would never end, it must do, eventually. They were close to the shore, and there was a manned lighthouse on the Farnes. Once it was daylight, someone was bound to spot them.

Gradually, as the tide fell, the movement of the wrecked after-part of the ship became less violent. The thumping, groaning and screeching as the sea battered it died away until finally it lay there motionless.

As soon as he judged it safe to do so, the third mate persuaded the passengers (there were nine of them – eight men and one woman) to climb down a rope ladder he had lowered on to the reef. Again he told them that at dawn, which couldn't be far off now, they were bound to be seen, either from the shore or from the Longstone light-house. The survivors, too numb and shocked to evince any reaction at all, huddled down on the rocks to wait for daybreak. . . .

For the Darlings in their lighthouse, it had been a very rough night. William Darling had been up most of the time, tending his light with extra care, knowing how much might depend upon it in such weather.

Grace slept, but was the first to wake in the morning. She was an early riser, and was always up and about soon after it had got light.

From habit, after a stormy night, she scanned the rocks and reefs around the lighthouse to check whether any vessel had come to grief there during the hours of darkness.

Suddenly she started, then called urgently to her father.

'Father! Father! There are people on Harcar!'

William Darling was quickly at her side with his telescope. He levelled it in the direction in which Grace was pointing, then, with a low exclamation, steadied it on one particular spot.

There were indeed people on Harcar, and there was wreckage strewn all around on the reef. Obviously a vessel of some size had struck there during the night.

Something had to be done about those people, and quickly too. William Darling knew that, in that kind of weather, it was as easy to die from exposure as from drowning, if not easier. They needed to be dry and warm at the earliest possible moment.

He sized up the situation. The weather was still extremely bad, and with the wind in that quarter there would be such a build-up of giant breakers on the coast that it would be almost if not wholly impossible for the lifeboat to put out. But what alternative was there?

Only one – that he should row across there himself. But could he do it? The sea between the lighthouse and the people marooned on the reef was not quite as rough as it was along the coast, and his intimate knowledge of the area would permit him to take advantage of every scrap of lee there was. On the other hand, his boat – it was a 6·5-metre rowing boat of a type known in those parts as a coble – was heavily built, and he was no longer a young man. What he really needed was another pair of hands at the oars.

It was then that Grace said, almost as though she had read his thoughts, 'I'll come with you, father.'

William Darling hesitated. His immediate impulse was to refuse. He loved his daughter dearly, and it would be a very dangerous thing he was committing her to, in more ways than one. There was not only the danger from the sea. Grace was very slight and delicate, and such an ordeal might easily overtax her strength.

But he also knew that she could handle a boat better than most men, and that when she had set her heart on doing something, especially something for other people, it was very hard to stop her.

His thoughts went back to the castaways on the reef. They must be wet, cold, frightened, and half-drowned. One or more of them could be injured, perhaps seriously. Getting them off as soon as possible could well be a matter of life or death. In any case something had to be done before the tide rose again.

Grace's mother begged her not to go, but she too knew that the girl would do what she felt she must.

Minutes later the lighthouse keeper and his daughter were on their way. The coble reared and plunged madly in the heavy seas, but the two of them rowed steadily, unhurriedly, keeping perfect time with each other, as they had done so many times before.

They reached the reef safely. Eight men and one woman were huddled, shivering, there. One of the men was injured.

William Darling jumped ashore. Grace tended the tossing boat while the casualty was lifted into it. The coble had to make two trips to take all the survivors off. On the first it took the woman, who had, tragically, lost two children in the wreck, and four of the men. Two of these men went back with Grace's father on the second trip to fetch the other four.

Altogether, thirty-eight men and women were lost in the wreck of the *Forfarshire*. Nine were saved from the sea, thanks largely to the courage of a girl called Grace Darling.

After the rescue, Grace was, deservedly, the most famous young woman in Britain. She was awarded a grant of £50 by the British government of the day in recognition of her bravery, and this was greatly augmented by a sum of £750 which was collected for her by public subscription. Her father received £270, and both he and Grace were awarded the gold medal of the Humane Society.

Grace Darling's life was all too short. Never strong, she became an invalid shortly after she had done her great deed. She died of tuberculosis, one of the great scourges of those days, at the sadly early age of twenty-seven.

Operation Capsize

Saturday, 19th September, 1964 was a normal sort of day at Tangalooma, a seaside resort near Brisbane, which is the chief city of Queensland, Australia. The sun was hot, and the beach crowded with sun-tanned bodies. The blue sea was dotted with swimmers and surf-riders.

A lifeguard on the beach was keeping an eye on what was going on. Suddenly, as he swept the sea with his powerful binoculars, he checked.

'Hey!' he called to his companions. 'There's someone out there – way out there!'

'You mean someone swimming?' one of the other lifeguards asked.

'Yeah! And he's waving. He's in trouble!' The lifeguard lowered his binoculars. 'Let's go get him!'

A boat was quickly launched and headed seaward, driven swiftly by a powerful outboard motor. The men in the boat were puzzled. Where on earth could the swimmer have come from? He certainly hadn't swum out from the beach – they'd have seen him if he had. And there was nowhere out there except the Pacific Ocean, with South America a few thousand kilometres away.

The boat reached the man just in time. Another few minutes and it would have been too late. Grey in the face, eyes staring, he hung on to the gunwale.

'Men!' he gasped out. 'Men drowning! Moreton Bay!'

They got him into the boat, and when he had recovered a little, he told them who he was. They knew already from his accent and limited vocabulary that he wasn't a native Australian.

He told them that his name was Erik Poulsen, and that he was Danish, one of the crew of the *Captain Neilsen*, a dredger which had been working in Moreton Bay.

At that point he became agitated again.

'Capsized!' he shouted. 'Ship capsized. All men trapped inside!'

The boat was already heading for the shore. As it covered the rest of the distance, Poulsen's rescuers got as much more information from him as they could, considering his condition. Apparently the *Captain Neilsen* had been working normally when suddenly, without warning, she had turned turtle. As far as Poulsen knew, he was the only member of her crew that had got away from her. He had swum clear, and, when it had become obvious that there was nothing he could do on the spot, had started swimming towards the coastline he could see some kilometres away. When his rescuers told him what time it was, he said he reckoned he must have been in the water about three hours.

The boat grounded on the beach and, while a couple remained behind to look after Poulsen, the rest of the men dashed off to get a rescue operation underway. That proved more difficult than it might have been at another time because it was the week-end, and suitable people who might otherwise have been at work and therefore readily available had gone away till Monday. However, after a great deal of activity, including a lot of telephoning, a varied rescue crew was got together, which included both professional divers and members of Brisbane's skin-diving clubs.

The party set out in a number of motor dinghies, heading for Moreton Bay, while a helicopter went ahead to locate the wreck.

It wasn't hard to find. In the prevailing conditions of good visibility, the *Captain Neilsen* was just too big to miss. She was large for a dredger, around three thousand tonnes, and she was lying on the surface like some enormous basking whale.

The chopper directed the boats to the wreck. They went alongside, and the rescue party scrambled on to the hull. Poulsen had insisted on going along, and was one of the first to jump on to the barnacle-encrusted, rust-streaked plates. He had taken a hammer with him, and began banging hard on the steel.

It was the classic make-or-break situation in mishaps of that kind. Would there be an answer? The steel rang under Poulsen's urgent, anxious blows, which meant there was air inside the hull. If it had been full of water, the sound would have been dead.

So would the men – but they weren't. Suddenly, after a tense wait which must have been much shorter than it seemed, there came answering bangs from inside the ship.

Poulsen turned to the others, his face alight with joy.

'They are alive!' he shouted. 'Alive!'

'How many?' the leader of the team asked him.

'Twenty-four,' Poulsen said. 'Twenty-four in the crew, without me.'

'You think they're all in there?'

'Perhaps. I think so.'

There was now the problem of rescue. To cut a hole in the hull would have been fatal, since that would have released the air which was keeping the *Captain Neilsen* afloat.

There was only one thing to do, and that was to go down, under and up.

'If we can get in,' the leader of the party said, 'we can bring them out one by one.'

The operation was begun at once, but almost immediately ran into a snag. The first diver to get under and into the ship returned to the surface to report that he had found his way barred by a steel door which was apparently secured on the other side. To get through it they would need underwater cutting gear.

The situation at once became very much more urgent. Obtaining the necessary equipment meant a trip ashore and back. How long would that take? And how long would the men's air last out? How long would the *Captain Neilsen* stay afloat? There was no guarantee that she wouldn't sink at any moment. How long would it take to cut through the door – and, if they managed that, might there not be similar obstacles behind it?

There was only one thing to do, and that was to get on with it. One of the boats headed shorewards at top speed to fetch the cutting gear, while the rescuers on the spot explored every other possible way of getting into the ship. After that they just waited, 'talking' to the imprisoned men with the hammer to keep their spirits up. In spite of their best efforts, however, the response of the trapped crew became more and more strained, and so did the nerves of the rescuers. Heads constantly turned shorewards to see if the boat was coming back.

It came at last, with its precious cargo. The cutting gear was heavy, and there were problems in getting it down and into the required position. Operating it was also difficult. It was exhausting work and the divers could only take short turns at it. While they were working, relays of skin divers maintained a keen-eyed patrol around the vessel, for these were shark-infested waters.

The cutting job went on, and as it did so a further anxiety arose. As the slit in the steel door grew longer, more and more water was getting through into the previously air-tight space beyond. At what level would the flooding stop? The work with the oxy-acetylene torch was irrevocable – once it was done, there was nothing to stop the influx of the sea. The rescuers might even be drowning the men they were trying to save, but there was nothing else they could do. They could only hope and pray, and go on working as hard as was humanly possible.

Cutting through the heavy steel door took ten hours, during which time the tireless Poulsen never stopped 'talking' to his shipmates with his hammer, encouraging them over and over again to hang on just a little longer. He kept up a running commentary on what the rescuers were doing, and told the men in the hull not to worry. Things were going fine! The door must give at any moment now! Just a few more minutes and they would be safe!

At last the great moment came. One of the divers surfaced, and he was not alone. He was supporting one of the dredger's crew.

The other divers instantly went down and, one by one, fifteen of the *Captain Neilsen*'s crew were brought up.

The others lost their lives. Two of them were in a part of the ship from which they couldn't have been rescued in those circumstances, even if they were alive, which was doubtful. And Erik Poulsen had been wrong in thinking that 'all men' had been in the ship. It was established later that the others had been lost at the time of the capsize.

The fact remains that more than half the *Captain Neilsen*'s complement had been saved from the sea – and by a Saturday afternoon rescue party at that. It was dramatic proof that, even when unlimited equipment and highly organised teams of experts weren't available, courage and co-operation could go a long way towards doing as good a job.

The Spare Man

The little Cornish town of St Ives is a picturesque place. The old houses around its tiny harbour are Mediterranean in colour and in the way they are jumbled together, and so are the bright fishing boats that lie there. Nearby are wide, sweeping beaches of dazzling white sand. On a hot, sunny day it is easy to think you are on the French or Italian riviera rather than in south-west England.

But in winter, when the winds reach gale force, the picture is a very different one. St Ives is on the north coast of that long, narrow, spiny promontory which ends in the blunt and beetling cliffs of Land's End, and when the great south-westerlies blow and huge seas come roaring in with the weight of the whole Atlantic Ocean behind them, the pretty rocks and beaches become a cruel lee shore. Woe betide any vessel that is storm-driven on to that shore!

It goes without saying that St Ives is a very important lifeboat station. Her lifeboat's crew has some of the toughest of all life-saving jobs to do. And their lives are in hazard even more than those of many of their colleagues elsewhere around our coasts.

On the night of 24th January, 1939, the west of England was battered by a storm of unprecedented violence. Even the oldest inhabitants of the town couldn't remember anything like it. The local coastguard station recorded wind gusts of over 150 kilometres per hour, and offshore there was foam-streaked, roaring chaos.

Many of the locals, wise in the ways of the sea, reckoned a lifeboat call was inevitable. . . .

It came shortly before midnight, when distress signals were seen about a mile out to sea from the Pendeen light. Within minutes the warning maroons had sounded, and the lifeboat's crew was racing for the harbour.

This was her regular crew, apart from one man. He was sick, but arrangements had been made for someone to take his place. The replacement, or 'spare man', was Will Freeman, who was being thrown in at the deep end with a vengeance. It would be the first time he had served in the lifeboat's crew, and he was not likely ever to forget it.

The lifeboat was the *John and Sarah Eliza Stych*. She was a splendid boat with powerful engines, and the man in command of her, Coxswain Thomas Cocking, had great confidence in her – as his crew had in him. If there was anywhere a more seaworthy vessel or a more capable coxswain, it was hard to imagine it.

A small crowd had gathered to watch the launch, standing hunched against the wind which was so strong that it took more than seventy men to get the boat into the water.

The lifeboat's engines roared into life and, with her crew of eight, including the spare man, she headed out into the heaving, foam-streaked blackness beyond the harbour entrance. The minute she left the shelter of the harbour wall she was lifted high and dizzily by a giant wave, and from then on being aboard her was like riding on a crazy roller-coaster.

The vessel in distress was believed to be about twenty kilometres west along the coast, and Coxswain Cocking headed the *John and Sarah Eliza* in that direction. It wasn't very far to go, but the wind was so strong and the seas so enormous that after a while he began to wonder if even his splendid boat could make it.

Progress was extremely slow, and they had made only a couple of kilometres when a terrible thing happened. Every time the boat reared up on the crest of a great wave, the wind struck savagely at her, trying to force her bows round. The coxswain, wrestling with the wheel, did his best to hold her up to the weather, but there came a time when it proved more than he could manage. As the lifeboat rose yet again to the foaming crest of a giant hill of water, the wheel was snatched from his hands. The boat fell off the wind, crabbing sideways, and dropped broadside on into the deep trough beyond. The next huge sea rolled her over.

The *John and Sarah Eliza* was a marvellous sea boat. She was self-righting, and within seconds she was on an even keel again – or as even as it was possible to be, in the circumstances. But of the eight men she'd had on board, four, including the coxswain, were missing. Two of the remaining four had been washed overboard, but had managed to hang on to the lifelines. Their shipmates pulled them back on board. One of the two was the spare man, Will Freeman.

Power was off, and the boat was wallowing, at the mercy of wind and sea. The gale, blowing hard on-shore, was driving her nearer and nearer to the cruel rocks of the coast.

Richard Stevens, the lifeboat's mechanic, managed to restart the engines. The *John and Sarah* was under way again. But in those extraordinary conditions, and after the loss of their comrades, going on with the rescue attempt was out of the question. They had more than enough to do to save themselves. The only sensible thing would be to turn and head for home.

The lifeboat's bows swung off the wind again, but by intent this time and at a carefully chosen moment. She heaved and wallowed beam-ends on, but she got round safely and headed back the way she had come.

But it was far from being just a case of running back. In fact this was a more dangerous course than the one she'd been on before. As with any boat, it was even harder to steer her when she was driving before the weather than when she was punching into it. As each great sea overtook her and lifted her stern high, her rudder became temporarily useless. Also, her propeller had been damaged, which cut her power and cost her steerage-way. Every wave that passed under her threatened to throw her stern round, slew her sideways, and swamp her.

Somewhere ahead lay St Ives Bay, the harbour, and safety. But where? The night was so dark that the men in the boat could scarcely see each other even in the vaguest outline, let alone anything further away. The boat had a compass, of course, but with her veering so wildly from side to side it was impossible to steer by it.

But seeing or being seen was vital, the more so as they got nearer the land. They lit a number of the red distress flares the lifeboat carried. They were seen from the shore, but there was nothing anyone there could do.

To try to control the boat's rolling a little, they rigged the tough

59

storm trysail to her stumpy mast, but it was blown out almost at once.

Then the men's worst fear was realised – she broached to. As she slid down one of the huge, steep seas, her stern swung round, and, while she lay broadside-on, the next wave burst roaring over her, turning her over a second time.

Again she righted herself, but by the time she had done so, another of her crewmen had disappeared. The three that were left could only continue to cling on for their lives while the lifeboat, completely out of control, reared and dropped dizzily, driven helplessly shorewards before the storm.

She was doomed, and so were the men in her. There could be little doubt about that. Near the shore the bay was a mass of leaping breakers and seething, roaring foam. No vessel, not even a lifeboat, could hope to live in that. And there was no way of avoiding it. The wind was driving the boat inexorably in that direction.

Will Freeman was one of the three men left in the boat. His main reaction to having survived so far was one of surprise. Now, like the other two, he could only hang on and wait. None of them thought they'd be lucky a third time. Sooner or later, if she wasn't over-whelmed before then, the *John and Sarah Eliza* must run aground, either on one of the sandy beaches or on the rocks at the far side of the bay. It didn't much matter which. Neither the boat nor the men in her could hope to come through the pounding they would surely get then.

Suddenly one of the other two men shouted.

'Look out! Wave!'

Looking up, Will Freeman saw a huge sea towering over him in the darkness. It seemed to hang poised for an eternity, then fell on the boat. The lifeboat capsized a third time, and for a third time righted herself.

But there was only one man in her now. He had been hurled roughly to the floorboards, and as he lay there had seen his remaining two shipmates swept away. He had heard their shouts as they were lost in the engulfing night.

Minutes later, the boat struck. The rough rhythm of the surging seas gave way to a whirlpool of confused water, and suddenly there was a terrifying crash, followed by loud scraping and rending noises.

The sole survivor of the *John and Sarah Eliza* lost consciousness then, and he must have remained in that condition for several hours. When he came to, everything was blessedly peaceful. The storm had blown itself out.

The lifeboat was lying high and dry on the rocks of Godrevy Point, on the eastern side of St Ives Bay, where the ebbing tide had left it.

The man in her got to his feet and climbed out on to the rocks through a huge hole in the boat's port side. Weeping with a combination of relief and sheer exhaustion, he dragged himself up the rocks. When, some time later, he came to a cottage, he had just enough strength left to knock at the door.

The one survivor of the *John and Sarah Eliza Stych* was Will Freeman, the spare man, who had been saved not so much from as by the sea.

The Desert Castaways

It was 29th November, 1942. The 11,000-tonne Blue Star liner *Dunedin Star* was making her way down the west coast of Africa. Her lights were screened and she was steaming as close to the shore as possible. This was the third year of World War Two, and there were U-boats abroad in the Atlantic. The *Dunedin Star* had to take extra care because she was not in convoy. She was steaming alone.

The ship was already a war veteran. In September 1941 she had made the hazardous trip through the western Mediterranean to deliver supplies and personnel to the besieged island of Malta. For this gallant exploit her captain and chief engineer had been awarded the O.B.E. and her chief officer the M.B.E.

It was late that November night when the radio station at Walvis Bay, a seaport some 650 kilometres further down the coast, picked up an S.O.S. message to the effect that the *Dunedin Star* had struck a submerged object, and that she was steaming at full speed for the land, to beach herself.

The *Dunedin Star* was three weeks out from Liverpool, en route for the Middle East, via Cape Town, with military supplies. With the Axis powers dominating the Mediterranean, it was no longer feasible for merchant ships to go that way. Instead they had to make the long haul round the Cape of Good Hope.

The liner had over a hundred people on board, some of them passengers, including women and children. Almost everyone, except for members of the crew who were on watch, had turned in and was asleep when the collision occurred.

What was it? What had they hit? The look-outs hadn't seen anything. It must have been something submerged, and, whatever it was, something very big and very solid. The fact that there were three 'bumps', the first extremely heavy and the other two less so, suggested that the ship had run on to a reef. The most likely explanation was that she had hit the Clan Alpine Shoal, which lies some eight kilometres off the coast of South West Africa.

The captain's natural reaction after the impact was to alter course away from the coast, to get out into deeper water. But then reports were made to him that the ship was badly damaged. The engine room and two of her holds were taking in so much water that she was in grave danger of sinking.

The captain looked bleakly at his chief engineer. He said, 'How long do you think we can stay afloat?'

The chief engineer shook his head. 'Not long, sir. I'd say three or four hours, not more.'

'Then there's only one thing for it. We'll have to put her on the beach.'

The *Dunedin Star* altered course again, this time towards the land. It was an odd feeling, steaming more or less blind—towards what? The night was overcast and very dark, with no moon or stars, and to make things worse the ship's depth-sounding gear had been damaged when she struck, so there was no way of telling how much water she had under her.

What lay ahead? Another reef, on which she might tear her bottom out? Or was she going to run slap into cliffs?

In the event, she was lucky. After a while the anxious men on her bridge heard the roar and saw the pale loom of breakers in front of her bows. The captain reduced speed, and minutes later the ship ran on to a very gently shelving, sandy beach. As she grounded, she swung broadside-on, heeling to starboard towards the big, foaming seas running in.

She was safe for the moment, but she had got there only just in time. Her engine room floor was awash. Only a little longer and she would have had no power to drive her.

When the ship struck the first time, her lifeboat drill had come into operation, but after a while the passengers had been told to return to their cabins. They were now called out again, with their lifebelts, and requested to stand by. They were informed that there was no immediate danger, and that no further move would be made until daylight.

The *Dunedin Star*'s predicament was nevertheless frightening enough. Huge waves were breaking over her amidships, and the water in her engine room was getting deeper all the time. Shortly after midnight this part of the ship had to be evacuated, which meant that, since she was a motor vessel and all her auxiliary machinery was electrical, all her lights went out.

There she lay, a dark and apparently lifeless hulk, until dawn revealed her situation. She had run aground on a shallow coast where rows of huge breakers came roaring in for as far as the eye could see. The shore itself was low and featureless, just a long line of sand dunes with, apparently, no vegetation at all.

Meanwhile there had been a reply to the ship's S.O.S. call, but it wasn't an entirely encouraging one. Walvis Bay was sending a tug and a trawler to the *Dunedin Star*'s assistance, but it would take them at least two days to get there.

The S.O.S. had also been received by other ships in the area, and two of them, the British freighter *Manchester Division* and the Norwegian motor vessel *Temeraire*, replied saying that they were turning off-course and would take off the *Dunedin Star*'s passengers. But again it would be a couple of days before either arrived.

The captain of the *Dunedin Star* decided that that was too long to wait. Because the ship was obstructing the normal sweep of the waves, sandbanks were building up on either side of her amidships, and at the same time the sea bed was being scoured away under her bow and stern. She was rolling, bumping and straining all the time, aground only in the middle. With her extremities unsupported, she could easily break in two.

The captain's first responsibility was to his passengers, and he realised that something must be done about them with a minimum of delay. He simply couldn't afford to wait until the rescue vessels arrived and took them off.

The obviously desirable thing was to get them safely on to dry land, and after some thought he decided to attempt to land both passengers and crew in the ship's motor boat. As a safety precaution extra supplies of food, water and medical equipment were stowed in the boat. He considered that a free run in to the beach would be too

hazardous – any one of those great rollers could swing the boat broadside and overwhelm it, in which event most if not all of those in it would almost certainly drown. The boat was therefore to be paid out on the end of a rope, to keep it end-on to the breakers.

The boat wasn't very large, so it would mean making several trips. The first boatload got ashore safely, though drenched to the skin, but the rudder fastenings were damaged as the boat grounded heavily on the hard sand. This meant that new fittings would have to be made, which in turn meant delay.

When the damage had been repaired, two more trips were made successfully, but on the third the sea hurled the boat savagely on to the beach, completely wrecking it. By great good luck there were no casualties.

There were now sixty-three people, including eight women and three babies, stranded on the beach, with no shelter and only the supplies brought ashore by the now useless motor boat to sustain them. What was more, this was one of the most empty and desolate stretches of coast in the world. They were marooned at a spot where a great stretch of desert came down to the sea. There was no vegetation, no habitation, virtually no life of any kind, for hundreds of kilometres both up and down the coast and inland, while to seaward there were those huge, interminably marching waves with the whole weight of the Atlantic Ocean behind them.

All the passengers were now on dry land, and some of the crew, but there were still forty-three officers and men on the ship, which was being slowly pounded to pieces five hundred metres off-shore.

It quickly became apparent that one of the chief troubles of the people ashore was going to be exposure to sun and wind, and in particular to the fine, blowing sand, picked up by the wind off the beach, which got into the eyes, nose and mouth and made life a misery. The chief officer, who was among those who had got ashore, took charge and set up a camp on the lee side of a sand dune some two hundred metres from the edge of the sea. The motor-boat had auxiliary spars and sails, and these were used to rig makeshift tents for as many of the women and children as could be crowded into them. The rest of the castaways, for the time being at any rate, had to take their chance in the open.

Some of the castaways went off to look for fresh water. They didn't find any, but they did come across the ribs of an old sailing ship, with some huts on the shore nearby. They also found some human bones, which, in the circumstances, was not a very encouraging discovery. The curious fact that there were no skulls among the bones didn't make them feel any easier either.

The next forty-eight hours passed without very much change in the situation. The Norwegian motor vessel *Temeraire* put in an appearance at dusk on the second day and anchored five kilometres away from the *Dunedin Star*. The British ship *Manchester Division* arrived later that night.

Next morning the *Temeraire* sent a boat with a volunteer crew to try to take some of the remaining crewmen off the Blue Star vessel. A heavy swell, with many of the waves breaking into surf, made the operation an extremely tricky one, but ten men were taken off and put on board the *Manchester Division*, which was easier for the laden boat to reach than the *Temeraire*. Encouraged by this initial success, the *Temeraire*'s boat managed to get everyone else off in the course of the morning. The *Dunedin Star*'s captain, chief engineer and another engineer were put on board the tug *Sir Charles Elliott*, which had now joined the other vessels at the scene of the stranding.

The minesweeper *Nerine* arrived from Walvis Bay next day. There was still too much surf running for the rescue vessels to be able to do anything about the castaways ashore, and by now the little *Sir Charles Elliott* was running short of coal, so she transferred the *Dunedin Star*'s captain and engineer officers to *Nerine* and steamed off back to port. Since it didn't seem there was much else she could do, the *Temeraire* also left. *Nerine* and *Manchester Division* stayed on.

By this time the castaways were beginning to suffer from exposure. The days were extremely hot and the nights correspondingly cold, so that those on the open beach were being alternately scorched and frozen. And the sand was a never-ending problem. It got in everywhere, whatever precautions were taken against it.

The outlook wasn't very bright. No rescue would be possible from seaward while the surf was running as high as it was now, and there was no telling how long it might go on like that. It was in fact the normal state of the sea on the coast. And there was little hope of help arriving overland for at least some considerable time.

Late that afternoon the British freighter *Manchester Division* passed to the people on the beach by signal lamp the cheering news that a bomber was being sent from Cape Town, more than 1500 kilometres away, to drop them supplies, and also that an overland rescue party had set out from the South African frontier town of Windhoek. This party was travelling in a convoy of eight vehicles which included a repair van, a water trailer, and an ambulance.

Not to be outdone, the minesweeper *Nerine* moved closer to the beach, and made an attempt to float rafts stocked with food and water ashore. It was a good idea, in theory, but in practice it didn't work. A strong current carried the rafts away northwards along the coast.

The promised bomber, which belonged to the Royal South African Air Force, left Cape Town soon after dawn on 3rd December. It stopped en route at Walvis Bay, and not long after resuming its flight its crew spotted a vessel stranded on the coast with great seas washing over her.

It wasn't the *Dunedin Star*, whose reported position was another sixty-five kilometres to the north. It was the tug *Sir Charles Elliott* which, on her way back to Walvis Bay, had run aground at six o'clock that morning. Much smaller than the *Dunedin Star*, she was far more vulnerable to the huge waves pounding her, and was rapidly breaking up. Two of the men on her were drowned trying to get ashore.

A few minutes later the plane sighted the *Dunedin Star* and the castaways' camp. Running in low over the camp, it dropped food and water and medical supplies from a height of about five metres. The food and medical supplies, which were strongly boxed, landed safely, but most of the water cans burst. A further 150 litres of water were dropped safely on a second run.

The pilot of the bomber, Captain Naude, then decided to risk a landing to pick up as many of the passengers as he could take, the women and children and anyone sick having obvious priority. He had spotted a level stretch of sand about three kilometres inland which looked as though it might serve as a landing strip and put the twelve-tonne aircraft down there safely, but then it got bogged down while taxiing. The combined efforts of her crew of four, plus five of the castaways who, seeing the plane landing, had come hurrying over from their camp, could not budge her.

There were now three casualties on that forbidding stretch of coast: the *Dunedin Star* herself, the tug *Sir Charles Elliott* and the plane.

Nerine had to leave next day for Walvis Bay, to refuel and replenish her stores. With her she took the *Dunedin Star*'s captain, much against his will. He would far rather have been put ashore so that he could assume direct responsibility for the passengers and crew in the camp, but in the prevailing sea conditions that was something that simply could not be done.

Nerine was nothing if not a tryer. Before she left she made another attempt to float food and water ashore on a raft. This, like its predecessors, was carried away up the coast, but this time the operation wasn't in vain. The raft was tracked by a number of the castaways and eventually recovered, with some of the earlier ones, some ten kilometres away. Some of the containers were too heavy to carry, but at least the stores were there. The castaways took back all they could carry, and from then on they had no real worry about supplies.

Late that same day another minesweeper, the *Natalia*, left Walvis Bay to stand by in *Nerine*'s place. The following day a second bomber from Cape Town made drops at both the *Sir Charles Elliott* and *Dunedin Star* camps. As before, much of what was dropped was spoiled, but a certain amount was picked up in a usable condition.

The next three days saw a good deal of activity. A plane located the rescue party which was trekking overland, and of which nothing had been seen or heard since it had started out. And the crew of the *Sir Charles Elliott*, luckier than the survivors of the *Dunedin Star* in that they had terrain suitable for a runway not too far away, were air-lifted to safety.

On 9th December the minesweeper *Nerine* returned and dropped anchor as close to the shore as she dared. With her she had brought a surf boat and experts to man it. She was going to make another attempt to get at least some of the people off the beach. To do this, one of the *Dunedin Star*'s lifeboats was lowered and anchored 150 metres off-shore, and attempts were made to fire a light line from the boat to the beach. Each time the line fell short, and in the end a young sailor volunteered to swim ashore with the line, and did so success-fully. Some of the men on the beach then hauled in a heavier hawser to establish an escape route between the beach and the lifeboat. One of the men ashore pulled himself hand over hand along the hawser to the lifeboat, and in due course fourteen other men followed his example.

But there were others of the castaways who couldn't be expected to attempt such a vigorous and dangerous way of escape, and this was where the surf boat came in. The surf boat was allowed to drift in to the beach on a line from the lifeboat, and was hauled off again with the eight women and three babies in it. It had a very rough passage. Half way out a breaker very nearly filled the boat, and, just as it came alongside the lifeboat, another wave capsized it and threw everyone in it into the sea. Two of the women and two babies were dragged into the lifeboat, but the rest were washed overboard and eventually ashore. By a miracle, no lives were lost, but the surf boat was a write-off. It was later thrown up on the beach, shattered and useless.

Altogether, nineteen of the castaways reached *Nerine*, where they were given hot food and drink and put to bed.

During the night the wind strengthened and the surf became much worse. Rescue from the beach would have been impossible in such conditions. Luckily things improved next day sufficiently to allow another eleven of the castaways plus two of the crew of the *Nerine* who had been landed the day before to haul themselves off to safety. That evening the minesweeper sailed for Walvis Bay with twenty-six survivors on board.

Meanwhile the attempt to reach the castaways overland had run into trouble. The trans-desert convoy had to combat not only sand and very rough going over uneven ground, but fog. Its difficulties had indeed become so great that a second convoy had set out to back up the first.

On 12th December a reconnaissance plane reported that the second convoy was sixty-five kilometres behind the first, which hadn't done so badly after all. It was now only ten kilometres from the castaways' camp.

There was a great moment round about five o'clock that afternoon when two members of the first convoy, trudging ahead, reached the camp. The convoy itself settled down for the night without attempting to cover the last few kilometres. Next day, all the men in the castaways' camp who were fit enough walked the ten kilometres to the convoy park. A truck fetched the others.

On 14th December the convoy set out for the nearest point from which the survivors of the *Dunedin Star* could be airlifted out. As on the outward trek, conditions were terrible, with torrential rain most of the way. But they made it in two days. On 16th December an aircraft took off with fourteen of the survivors on board, including six women and a baby. There were nearly two babies – one of the women was pregnant, and her child was born next morning.

Having landed this first batch, the plane returned to pick up the rest of the passengers and six of the *Dunedin Star*'s crew who were in need of medical attention. One of the passengers, whose appetite for adventure was apparently not yet fully satisfied, said he'd rather stay with the convoy, so the plane left him behind.

It was just after noon on Christmas Eve when the eleven trucks of the convoy reached the South African town of Windhoek after a round trip of some 2400 kilometres.

Meanwhile a start had been made on tidying things up. Captain Naude's bomber was a valuable aircraft, and had to be recovered, if possible. There was also a great deal of salvagable material on the *Dunedin Star*.

On 17th December the minesweeper *Crassula* left Walvis Bay with a salvage party and their gear on board. The salvors managed to recover 300 tonnes of cargo and 4000 bags of mail which had been on its way to troops serving in the Middle East. Now it was on its way again. Some of the men in the front line were going to get their letters a little late, but where news from home was concerned, it was very much a case of better late than never.

On 17th January, 1943, an expedition set out from Windhoek to sort out the bogged-down bomber. With it went Captain Naude and two air mechanics. The expedition reached the plane on 26th January.

It had been decided that the only way the aircraft could take off would be by laying wire netting over the sand to form a runway. Two thousand metres of netting were transported to the spot and laid – an immense task in itself.

Now it only remained for Captain Naude to get the bomber into the air. He managed to do so successfully, and those watching breathed again as they saw the big plane steady on a course along the coast. It seemed the adventure was over at last.

It wasn't. At least it wasn't for Captain Naude and his men. The bomber was flying at 150 metres, following the coastline, when it developed engine trouble. Captain Naude decided that he would have to land, and that the best place to do so was in the shallow water close to the beach, but before he could put the plane down, it nose-dived into the surf 200 metres out, breaking up into three sections on impact.

By a miracle, no one was killed. The three men in the plane were badly hurt, Captain Naude the most seriously, but they all escaped with their lives and managed to get ashore, Naude with the help of the other two.

Their situation was grave. They managed to salve some emergency rations and a five-litre can of water from the plane, but they had no radio, and so no way of calling for help. In their injured condition they weren't very mobile, nor could they afford to wait very long for rescue.

It seemed to Captain Naude that there was only one thing for it, and that was for the least badly injured of them to try to intercept the expedition which had got them into the air, on its return journey.

The man in question set out, with the other two staggering after him. Three days later, by a great stroke of luck, the first man met the convoy, which had been delayed in starting back. He broke the news of the plane crash, and said that his two companions were following along somewhere behind him.

The adventure really was over then. It had been an extraordinary one, if only in that, with the exception of the two men of the crew of the *Sir Charles Elliott* who had been drowned, no lives had been lost. Ingenuity, courage and perseverance had brought a large number of people through many dangers and hardships to safety.

Fire Down Below!

It was a calm, clear evening in the summer of the year 1827. The passenger steamer *Clydesdale* was on her way down the river from which she took her name, bound for Ireland.

The Clyde, that fine, broad waterway which flows from the great Scottish port of Glasgow down to the Irish Sea, can be extremely dangerous in bad weather, especially in fog. That evening it was like a lake, and the barometer was high and steady. It never occurred to anybody on board the *Clydesdale* that a voyage in such conditions could be fraught with danger.

The tall-funnelled steamer cleared the entrance to the river and thumped her way peacefully, with her great paddles turning like mill wheels, out into the strait between Scotland and northern Ireland called the North Channel. Because it was such a fine evening there were more passengers out on deck than usual.

The man at the *Clydesdale*'s wheel was a tough and experienced Scot named Maxwell. Jim Maxwell had been piloting ships up and down the Clyde for years. He knew every rock and current and sandbank, every twist and turn of the channel along the great river's course. He knew as did very few others how to make the best possible use of the tides, and how to 'read' the local weather.

The *Clydesdale* thumped on. The land fell slowly away behind. The light was failing now, but there were still a lot of people on deck, enjoying the voyage too much to go below.

Maxwell suddenly sniffed the air. He could smell something. Something burning . . .

Fire? Fire on board? It was probably nothing. Perhaps the cook had scorched a pan, or burned the potatoes.

Jim Maxwell was taking no chances. Fire at sea was a terrible thing. Calling for someone to relieve him at the wheel, he went briskly off to report the smell to the skipper, Captain Turner.

The captain wasn't taking any chances either. He came back along the deck with Maxwell. He could smell it too. 'We've got to find out where it's coming from,' he said.

It didn't take them long. As they came abreast of the engine-room hatchway, they were met by a blast of furnace-like heat. Then, before there'd been time for them to make any further move, they heard the crackling of burning wood.

Suddenly the starboard side of the ship was alive with leaping, darting tongues of flame.

Captain Turner knew only too well where those flames were coming from. He dashed to the side of the ship and found his fears confirmed. The starboard paddle-box was ablaze.

It was as bad a place as could be for fire to break out. For one thing, it was very difficult to get at. And if the paddle-wheel itself was destroyed, or the heat caused it to seize up, the ship would be helpless.

'You'd better get back to the wheel,' Captain Turner told Maxwell. Then he called the rest of the crew together and told them what the situation was. 'Now – form a bucket chain, all of you,' he ordered them. 'We've got to get as much water on that fire as we can.'

The men formed a chain and emptied one bucket after another over the side. The amounts seemed pitifully inadequate.

Captain Turner watched until he was satisfied the crew were doing all they could. Then he went to Maxwell at the wheel.

'Put her up to full ahead,' he said. 'And steer the straightest course you can. Don't give her a degree either way.' Then he dashed back to the engine-room, to see what was happening there.

It was then that, for the first time in his sea-going career, Jim Maxwell deliberately disobeyed an order. By that time the ship was just about half-way to Ireland, and he was of the opinion that in the circumstances it would be wiser to turn round and go back. For one thing, they would then be going with what slight breeze there was, so there would be less movement of air to fan the flames. For another, if the weather did freshen during the next hour or two, as it often did after dark, it would do so from the west. If they turned round, they would be running before it instead of having to punch into it.

He put the wheel hard over. With smoke and flames pouring from her burning paddle-box, the *Clydesdale* thrashed round in a circle and headed back towards the Scottish coast.

One part of the order Maxwell did obey, and that was to signal for full speed ahead. The great paddles thrashed faster and faster, and as they did so the fire in the starboard paddle-box got correspondingly worse. It was as though the paddle itself was fanning the flames that were consuming it.

Meanwhile, down below the stokers were having a tough time. They were working in a frenzy to fuel the boilers in an atmosphere of heat and fumes that made it difficult to breathe without choking. The engines themselves were scorching to the touch.

It was hot everywhere below, and almost all the passengers were now on deck, many of them in their night clothes. They kept asking if the ship was going to sink. Panic began to spread.

Part of the deck itself was now on fire, so Maxwell ordered all the passengers up into the bows of the vessel. The artificial 'wind' created by the steamer's speed would blow the flames back, so they would be safest there.

Shortly after this Captain Turner came up from below and went to the wheel. He realised straight away that the ship was heading back the way she had come, but, though he wasn't a man to take it lightly if his orders were disobeyed, he took no action in the present circumstances. It was too late to alter course again anyway, and on reflection he had to agree that Maxwell had done the right thing. Apart from considerations of wind and weather, there was the question of what to do when they reached land. His intention had been to run his ship ashore at the first suitable spot on the coast of Ireland, but it would be easier to do that on the more familiar Scottish shore.

By this time the crew had been forced to give up their fight against the fire. One or two stalwarts wanted to carry on, but Captain Turner, realising this might easily lead to injury or even death without doing any good, ordered all the crew to join the passengers in the bows.

He ordered Maxwell to go too, and for the second time Maxwell disobeyed.

'I'm not budging,' he said. 'I'm the pilot of this vessel, and I'm going to pilot her till we've completed this voyage. If there's no one on the wheel, she'll just go round in circles until we're all burned to death – or drowned.'

The captain didn't argue. He knew, from the many trips he'd done with him, how obstinate Jim Maxwell could be.

The ship was steaming faster now than she had ever done in her life before. In order to get the absolute maximum out of her Captain Turner had ordered the shutting-down of the engine-room safety valves, even though that meant the boilers might burst.

Now the flames were licking around the wheel. Jim Maxwell shrugged his collar up against them and, steering with one hand, used the other to beat out the sparks that settled on his clothes.

His hands became painfully burned. In them rested the fate of the ship and everybody aboard her.

The engines rose to a new height of desperate endeavour. The paddle-wheels thumped faster and faster, as though the ship herself knew the danger she was in.

By this time the blaze had swept through the greater part of the vessel, devouring everything that would burn. Even the wheel was badly scorched. It seemed that it – and Jim Maxwell – might burst into flames at any time.

Maxwell still stuck to his post, though, with the fire so fierce and so close, his clothes had begun to smoulder. It became obvious that unless something was done he would be burned to death where he stood.

Captain Turner ordered the crew to form another fire-fighting chain. Buckets of sea water were drawn up, passed rapidly from hand to hand, and dashed over the brave helmsman. It was a crude but effective measure in that it enabled him to go on steering the ship.

The strange voyage continued. Not surprisingly, Jim Maxwell

said later that he felt it was going on for ever. He was alternately soaked to the skin and roasted by the fierce fire so perilously close to him, while the wreathing, thick black smoke made him choke and gasp for breath.

Captain Turner made several more attempts to persuade Maxwell to abandon the wheel, but met with no more success than he had done the first time. Maxwell did not even appear to hear. Maybe he was deafened by the roar and crackle of the flames.

The fire was still spreading, and the next development came when the stokers, who also had shown extreme bravery by continuing to do their job as best and for as long as they could in the circumstances, had to abandon the fire-filled engine-room. Cursing and sweating, they joined the others up in the bows of the ship.

By this time the *Clydesdale* had been spotted from the shore. A crowd had gathered and stood watching in fascinated horror as the ship steamed towards them, looking like a huge, flaring bonfire.

With the engines white hot and her boilers every moment more and more in danger of exploding, the steamer thrashed her way towards the land, with Maxwell still at the wheel. Though it was a miracle that he could even see, let alone stay where he was, he steered the ship skilfully through a narrow gap between rocks, and crashed dramatically on to a shingle beach. The spectators were forced back by the heat from the burning ship, but they quickly recovered themselves and dashed forward to help her crew and passengers to safety.

Jim Maxwell had suffered more than anyone else. The rescuers found him slumped across the wheel, his greatest feat of pilotage triumphantly accomplished. At first it was thought he was dead, but he wasn't. Though unconscious, he was still breathing.

He was borne gently away. As he was lifted from the wheel, his greatcoat fell to ashes around him.

Maxwell spent some time in hospital, but made a good recovery. He was back at sea again within a surprisingly short space of time.

'Maxwell the modest', as he became known, would never talk

about his exploit. But news of it spread far and wide in Scotland, and two substantial sums of money were raised for him by public subscription. Today he ranks as one of Scotland's greatest heroes of the sea.

The Overland Boat

A wild day was followed by a wilder night. The lifeboatmen of Whitby found it difficult to settle to anything that evening, or, later, to sleep. They had a sixth sense, born of experience, that they would be called out before daylight came.

Suddenly, above the shrieking of the wind and the dull booming of the surf on the shore and harbour walls, there sounded, high in the storm-torn blackness over the town, the flat, hard 'crack' of a signal rocket, known as a 'maroon' – the lifeboat alarm. A minute later there came a second burst of sound, emphasising the urgency of the first.

The men of the lifeboat's crew were on their feet in their various homes and struggling into their sea-going gear before the second maroon sounded. In a matter of minutes they were out of their cottages and running for the harbour, some of them still pulling on oilskins as they went.

Half the local population ran down to the harbour with them. Whitby was a seafaring town. It was from this little Yorkshire port that Captain Cook set sail on his voyage of discovery to Australia, and the cliff-top church of St Mary still has cabin-like windows, quarter-deck galleries, and a three-decker pulpit.

Whitby was also a fisherman's town and a busy little trading port. Almost everyone who lived there was connected with the sea in one way or another.

Men, women and children went streaming down to the harbour. They knew what it must be like at sea on a night like that, and whether the souls in distress out there were lost or saved was a matter of direct concern to them. It might easily be a Whitby boat that was in trouble. Someone in their own family – a son, a brother, or a husband – might well be in danger.

Then news came in that these fears were justified. As the lifeboat was wheeled out of its shed on its high carriage, the word spread that it was the Whitby brig *Visitor* that was in trouble.

'She's foundered,' one person told another, 'in Robin Hood's Bay.'

Then there were more details. 'The crew's got off in the ship's boat, but they can't get ashore in the sea that's running. Their only hope is to lie off and wait for the lifeboat.'

The crowd clustered round the lifeboat shed. Something was delaying the launch. Was there some trouble with the boat, or the launching ramp? Or perhaps they were waiting for some of the crew to arrive?

The real cause of the trouble was the weather. Robin Hood's Bay was ten kilometres to the southward along the coast, on the other side of the high cliffs of Ness Point, and with the wind coming from where it was, it would be quite simply impossible for the boat to reach her. This was the year 1881, when lifeboats were powered by sails and oars. To sail or row into the teeth of such a gale just couldn't be done by any boat's crew, however skilled, strong and brave they might be.

But men like the men of the Whitby lifeboat's crew didn't give up easily, especially when the lives of folk near and dear to them were in danger. Their one thought just then was that they had got to find some way of rescuing the crew of the stricken brig.

It was the lifeboat's coxswain who hit upon a way.

'Listen, lads!' he shouted above the roar of the storm. 'There's only one thing for it. We can't get there by sea, so we'll have to take the boat over the top!'

By 'over the top' he meant over the moorland road to Robin Hood's Bay. When he suggested it, it seemed a crazy idea, and the crowd's first reaction was to groan with incredulity and dismay. A woman in the crowd, the mother of one of the shipwrecked brig's crew, burst into tears. Robin Hood's Bay was all of ten kilometres away, and the road was steep and narrow. What was more, this had happened in the depth of winter, and the countryside was covered in snow. Up there on the open moors the gale would be blowing with

hurricane force, and anyone going to Robin Hood's Bay would have to battle right into the teeth of it.

But there were stout hearts who weren't prepared to dismiss the idea. If it was the only way, then they would have a try!

A sense of urgency came back. Two powerful draught-horses were sent for and came thundering down the narrow street to the harbour, striking sparks from the cobbles with their huge hoofs. They were quickly backed in and harnessed to the lifeboat carriage. There was a shout, and the horses strained against their traces. The lifeboat lurched and moved forward, with the crowd keeping pace with it on either side.

The rescue operation was under way. The lifeboat had been 'launched'.

There was trouble almost immediately. The road which led up out of the town was steep, and its cobbles were filmed with ice. The horses slipped and slid, splay-legged. The boat began to roll back.

Now it was the crowd's turn to do their bit. They grabbed the lifeboat's long hauling lines and tugged. Everyone who could get a hand on the line, including old men, women and children, set to and pulled their hearts out.

The lifeboat moved forward again. Slowly, lurching and slithering, it left the town behind.

The worst bit of all lay ahead. Conditions out in the country, up on the high moors, were frightful, far worse than the most pessimistic had feared.

But there was help there too. As the lifeboat jerked, crept and stopped, then jerked again and inched its way forward, a wayside farmer came out with another big draught-horse. Other farmers did likewise further on, until there was a great team of no less than fifty horses harnessed to the Whitby boat.

Progress was better now. There was literally plenty of 'horsepower' available, as well as the manpower of the crowd, and the operation had become organised. Teams of men went ahead to clear the worst snowdrifts, and the boat followed along the way they had opened up.

Then another obstacle arose. They came to a village with a street too narrow for the lifeboat to pass.

Having come so far, they weren't giving up now. The lifeboat coxswain went along the street knocking at the cottage doors. When the villagers heard what he wanted, they stared at him. The middle of a stormy winter's night is not the best time to have someone call and tell you he wants to knock part of your property down. But when they realised what was at stake, no one refused. Some even helped in the process of demolition.

The boat moved forward again between piles of rubble. It cleared the village. It reached a point on the open moor beyond which it was decided that it would be quicker and easier to leave the road and cut across country. The long line of horses veered off across the virgin snow.

The night was passing. A cold, grey dawn was breaking, and with it came the heartening news that the *Visitor*'s boat was still standing off, still riding out the weather. Everyone gave a great sigh of relief. The safety of the *Visitor*'s crew was still the object of this whole extraordinary operation. To have found the boat shattered on the rocky shore and one or more of its occupants drowned would have been too much to bear.

The road dipped steeply towards Robin Hood's Bay, and that posed another problem. So far the difficulty had been to keep the boat moving, whereas now the trouble was to stop it running away. The road was particularly slippery, glassy in fact, at this point.

The lead horse fell suddenly, neighing with terror. It was pulled to its feet again, but both it and the other horses had to be unharnessed and led aside. Their job, which they had done splendidly, was over.

It was up to the people now. The crowd took up the hauling lines once more, behind the boat this time, pulling back with all their might to brake its descent.

Slowly, slowly, the boat was eased down the road. It came to the little group of cottages that formed the community of Robin Hood's Bay. It was coaxed, pulled and shoved forward until at last it was down on the beach, with its bows pointing to the great breakers roaring in from seaward.

The prospect offshore was terrifying, but the lifeboatmen's spirits rose as many willing hands ran the boat out into the surf. This was their element. This was where they belonged, and what they understood. As soon as they were afloat, they bent to their oars with a will. The crowd on the shore stood watching, silent and motionless now, as the lifeboat was lost to sight in clouds of blinding spray. Would it make it? Or had all their efforts been in vain?

Time passed. It was wet and bitterly cold on the beach, with great sheets of spindrift slashing in as the giant breakers pounded the shore. But no one left to seek shelter. They were so committed now that they had got to stay there and see the rest of the drama played out, whatever the end might be.

More time passed. Many keen and anxious eyes searched the wild waste of waters that seemed to have swallowed up the lifeboat. The question was, could anything so small possibly survive in such seas?

Suddenly somebody shouted, 'There she is! There she is!'

And there the lifeboat was, a vague grey shape in the spume-filled, murky morning light. She was running swiftly in towards the beach, surfing high and fast on the foaming crests, with her crew rowing like mad to keep her end-on as the great breakers overtook and passed under her, then disappearing into the deep troughs beyond.

She came nearer and nearer. Now she was in the wild waste of water breaking on the beach. The men on the shore rushed into the sea, some of them waist-high, to drag her in.

The lifeboat's keel grated on the shingle. She was safe, and so was everyone in her.

A great cheer went up from the crowd as they saw how many men there were in the boat. The whole crew of the *Visitor* had been saved.

Adrift on a Raft

It must have been the change in motion that woke them. Instead of bobbing gently on its anchor rope, the raft was soaring and dropping dizzily. It was a wonder it hadn't tipped them off into the sea before now.

'Hey!' Frank Cushing said. 'What's happening?'

'We're drifting,' said his twenty-year-old son, Frank Junior, commonly known as 'Frankie'. 'We must be out at sea.'

Another great wave lifted them, and another. They were long and regular, deep-sea waves, which meant that, as Frankie had said, they must be out in the open ocean.

How far out? They had no way of knowing. They had no way of telling how long they had been adrift, except that the raft must have started moving some time during the night, and it was still dark. And, because it was dark, they had no idea in which direction the raft had been carrying them.

The two Franks, father and son, were mad about marine life, and on the night of 15th April, 1964, they had left on a trip to find specimens for their already impressive collection. They'd decided to make an overnight trip on their raft so that they would be at the place they wanted to dive when it got light.

Frank Senior had made the six-metre raft himself. It was merely a wooden platform supported by empty oil drums, but it served its purpose very well. All he and Frankie wanted was a diving platform, and it did admirably for that. Two outboard motors enabled them to move it from one diving point to another, which was all the mobility they needed.

The Cushings, who lived on the Pacific island of Guam, had boarded the raft the evening before and made a quiet trip to a peninsula called Pluto Point, where they had dropped anchor for a few hours' sleep. Whether it was because they did it in the dark, or were sleepy at the time, or for some other reason, they hadn't made a very good job of anchoring, and the raft had drifted free during the night.

All they could do now was wait for daylight. It came with the sun rising over a totally empty ocean. There was no land in sight anywhere.

Even then they didn't quite realise the fix they were in. They told themselves, and each other, they couldn't be all that far out. From their very low observation point on the raft, virtually at sea level, they had a horizon of only a few kilometres. They'd only got to head back in the right direction . . .

But which was the right direction? They had brought a small compass with them. They started the outboard motors, and the raft surged round until it was on what Frank Senior reckoned, or at least hoped, was a course which would take them back to land.

It required only a few minutes for it to become obvious that they were wasting their time. The raft had no great steering qualities or turn of speed even in calm water, and now, with each great wave checking it and throwing it off course, and with one or other of the outboard motor propellers, or sometimes both, racing in the air as a wave passed underneath, they were getting nowhere at all.

They were wasting not only time but fuel – fuel they might need later. They cut the motors, and all was silent, save for the hiss of the running seas.

All that day they drifted, without seeing anything at all. No land. Not a single ship or craft of any kind. Not even a seabird.

Frank Senior, who had a pretty good knowledge of winds and currents in that part of the world, reckoned they were heading for either the Philippines or China.

'Big deal,' Frankie said.

The sun set and it grew dark. The night passed with the raft continuing to soar and dip like some crazy roller-coaster as the waves passed under it, now and then tipping it sideways for good measure. At first they'd wondered how they were going to be able to stay on the thing for any length of time, but gradually they got used to it. They decided, when they got to that stage, that they ought to be all right for a while – at least as long as the weather remained fair.

Their spirits fell during the hours of darkness, but rose again when a new dawn came. They soared as a plane flew overhead. It was obviously searching for something, and they were pretty sure it must be them.

They made a smoke signal out of some petrol-soaked rag, but in spite of that the plane didn't see them. It flew on, and disappeared. They saw other planes later, but these didn't spot them either.

Darkness fell. They had another night to get through, and perhaps a good few more nights after that. If the air search hadn't found them that day, the odds against it happening next day or some time from then on would rapidly become so long as to be negligible. They had as little chance of being sighted by a ship. The hard fact of the matter was that they were drifting across one of the loneliest expanses of ocean in the world. Not that they were going to resign themselves to drifting helplessly. The two Franks just weren't that type.

Next day they set to work to do what they could to help themselves. They had two main objectives. They needed to get some idea of where they were, and some means of getting where they were going a bit quicker than they were doing at the moment. Frank Senior improvised a sextant out of a fish-spear prong and a length of fishing line, while Frankie devised a sail from blankets and some old parachute cloth.

The sail, rough and ready though it was, made a big difference. It drove the raft purposefully ahead, and it also exerted a steadying effect. It had a wonderful influence on its 'crew's' morale. The two Franks no longer felt themselves quite so much at the mercy of the ocean's waves and currents. They had a feeling that they were going somewhere definite, and that they were going to get there.

Their other two big problems were food and water. They had taken only just sufficient supplies on board to last them the short time they had expected to be at Pluto Point. They now divided what they had into the smallest daily amounts they thought they might survive on, but even then they could not expect to last very long merely on what they had.

Water was the real problem. They knew that if they had to, they could last a month or more without food, but, under that tropical sun, no more than four or five days without water.

Food never worried them at all. They could always catch fish. They spent a good part of each day fishing, and always caught more than enough for their needs. There were times, however, when they would have given anything for a change of diet.

Their water supply was getting scarce when, on the third day, Frank hooked a small dolphin. He killed it, and he and Frankie ate some of the dolphin's flesh. What was far more important, from its lungs they obtained something far more precious – fresh water. They kept the rest of the carcass for food.

Day after day the raft sailed on. When the sea got rougher, as it did several times, the two Franks lashed themselves to the raft and waited as patiently as they could for conditions to improve. Then, when they did, Frankie would go over the side with his skin-diving equipment.

These swims of Frankie's had two objectives. First, he checked that the oil drums supporting the raft were still in place and water-tight. Second, he was hunting for food. His father was to say later that it was Frankie's skill with his spear-gun that kept them both alive.

It was on one of these underwater hunts that Frankie got the shock of his life. He had gone quite deep and was swimming after a much bigger fish than usual when, happening to glance round, he saw a long, powerful, streamlined shape – a shark.

He straightaway forgot about the fish he'd been after. His one concern now was not to become the prey himself.

Then he got another shock. The shark wasn't alone. There was another only a few metres from the first, and just as big.

Frankie had his spear-gun, but he didn't for a moment kid himself that it would be any use against these formidable killers of the deep. There was only one thing for it, and that was to get back to the raft.

He flippered up as fast as he could, but that only attracted the sharks' attention. With what seemed like lazy flicks of their tails they came soaring effortlessly up out of the depths, moving at several

times his speed. They circled him, edging in closer all the time. They came so close that he could see their cold, staring eyes.

After what seemed like for ever, he broke surface, and being back in his own element of air gave him heart and renewed energy. But the raft was still some distance away.

Suddenly, with no warning at all, one of the sharks did a sharp turn and came straight at him. Frankie's one and only reaction then was that he must at all costs get away from it. He swam desperately for the raft, reached it, and grabbed at it. Looking up, he saw his father looming above him.

Frank Senior had a length of wood in his hand. Leaning over his son, he jabbed it down with all his strength. A dull thud as the wood struck flesh somewhere very near him told Frankie how close danger was.

With his father's help, he scrambled on to the raft. After a moment or two he sat up, gasping, safe but shaken.

'They're still with us,' Frank Senior said. 'There.'

He pointed. Frankie looked. The two sharks were swimming side by side a few metres behind the raft. Their lazy motions suggested infinite patience. They knew a good meal when they saw it, they seemed to say, and they were prepared to wait on the off-chance of enjoying it later.

Frank Senior took the opportunity of delivering a short lecture on sharks.

'You mustn't be afraid of them,' he told Frankie. 'In fact, there's no need to worry about them at all. If they get fresh, just bash them, and they'll go away.'

'Is that so?' Frankie said. He was still a bit white about the gills. He looked at the two sharks swimming patiently astern. 'You wouldn't care to give a demonstration?'

'The worst thing you can do is swim away from them,' his father said. 'If you do that, they'll think you're scared of them.'

'And they'd be darned right,' Frankie said.

'But if you go for them, then they're the ones that get scared.'

'At least that's the theory,' Frankie said. 'I'd still like to see you check it out.'

The sharks followed the raft for the rest of that day. But next morning they'd disappeared, and after a while the shock Frankie had suffered wore off. A day or two later, he had regained enough confidence to slip over the side again.

A few days after the first shark incident, a similar thing happened. Frankie spotted a shark and promptly made tracks for the raft, but he was still some distance from it when the shark turned and came at him. He obviously wasn't going to make it, so he waited until the shark was almost upon him, then drew up his knees and kicked out as hard as he could. He felt his feet thud into the shark's belly, and had the supreme satisfaction of seeing it turn smartly and swim away. From then on Frankie wasn't afraid of sharks, though he still treated them with respect, and kept clear of them if he could.

The strange voyage continued. By now the two Franks were almost resigned to its going on for ever. And they looked a couple of real sea-going castaways. They were unshaven and burnt by the sun, and their sun-bleached and salt-stained clothes were rapidly becoming rags.

But they had worked out a basic way of life that enabled them to exist. If nothing untoward happened, they could go on like that indefinitely, which meant that they had at least a chance of surviving. But something untoward did happen. . . .

Until now the Pacific had lived up to its name pretty well. There had been big seas running from time to time, but they had been regular and predictable. The weather had been set fair. Now something very different came along.

The first indication was a low black line on the horizon. At first Frank Senior thought it was what is called a 'line squall', which meant they would have to face a brief but violent change in the weather, with high winds, heavy rain, and rough seas. But he was wrong. As he and Frankie watched the line become more pronounced as it approached, they noticed that the sky above it stayed the same clear blue it had been ever since the start of their involuntary voyage.

Frank Senior suddenly realised what the black line was – a tidal wave. Somewhere, perhaps hundreds of kilometres away, there had been an upheaval of the sea bed which had thrown up the great ridge of water that was now rushing towards them.

They did the only thing they could, which was to lash themselves securely to the boards of the raft. Once separated from that flimsy platform, their lives would be numbered in hours, if not minutes.

The wave was approaching them at the speed of an express train. It was at least six metres high, and looked even higher because of the calmness of the water it was rushing across.

It reached them. It towered over them. The raft angled up the wave's steep forward side until it was hanging there almost vertically. Its timbers, which had never been intended to withstand anything like this, groaned and screeched as they worked against their fastenings. It seemed that the whole thing must disintegrate at any moment.

It didn't. It survived. It tilted on top of the wave, then slid at sickening speed down the other side.

The ordeal wasn't over yet. The first wave was followed by a second just as high. Once more the raft soared skywards, teetered crazily on the crest of the great, foaming hill of water, then slid down into the trough beyond.

There was a third wave, but it was much smaller than its two predecessors, and passed harmlessly under the raft.

For a while Frank Senior and his son just sat watching the triple hill of water speed on across the ocean – thankfully, away from them this time. They felt too limp to move.

'Well,' Frank Senior said at last, 'if that didn't get us, nothing will.' And he was right.

They set to and straightened up the raft. By that afternoon, things were back to normal. If you can call two sharks following astern 'normal'.

It was on 19th May, when they'd almost given up hope of ever doing so, that they saw land. For hours they steered towards it, and at last they reached it.

The excitement and joy they felt on making a landfall was premature. The island they had landed on was not only little more than a volcano – it was an active one.

There was no fresh water, so there was little point in staying. From the steep lava slopes they could see another island not far away. They relaunched the raft and made for that.

This second island had both drinking water and fresh fruit. They collected some of both, and settled down to what was surely the most marvellous meal anyone had ever eaten.

But they weren't allowed to enjoy this reward for all their long and lonely days at sea without interruption. As they sat on the beach, eating and drinking, a motor launch put in to the island. It was a Philippines coastguard vessel, and had been tracking them for a couple of hours on suspicion of being smugglers.

The launch took them back to its base, and they were flown out to civilisation. When they landed, they were fêted like heroes, but there was only one thing they wanted.

That was a good night's sleep, without having to worry about spearing fish, or squeezing water out of dolphins. Or sharks. Or tidal waves.

They had been on their home-made raft for thirty-five days.

Lifeline in the Sky

The message was dramatic: 'Portuguese ship *Arnel* aground and in danger of breaking up on shoals off Santa Maria. Women and children aboard. Surface vessels cannot assist – can you?'

The 'Santa Maria' referred to here was an island in the Azores, the Portuguese archipelago which lies far out in the Atlantic Ocean, roughly 1500 kilometres west of Portugal. The message, which came in by radio, was addressed to an American Air Rescue unit which had recently been set up on the island. The date was 19th September, 1958.

Within minutes one of the Air Rescue unit's helicopters was on its way to the scene of the stranding. It had a crew of three: the pilot, Captain Proctor; his co-pilot, Lieutenant Gagnon; and the hoist operator, Sergeant Monnie.

The Azores' normally good if somewhat boisterous weather had turned bad a day or two before. There had been a lot of rain with very high, squally winds that had gradually built up to the full gale that was now blowing.

The helicopter rose and fell with a sharp, jolting motion as it chopped its way through the turbulence. It was a bit like driving at speed along a very rough road. Heading well up to weather of his true course to allow for the drift caused by the gale, Captain Proctor felt the controls fighting him and knew that what lay ahead wasn't going to be easy.

It certainly wasn't. It was by far the most difficult job he'd ever had to do – one that called for every scrap of his skill and experience.

It was only about eight kilometres to the wreck and the helicopter found her easily enough. There she was, with a smother of white water surging over her.

The ship had gone aground in fog, and she had certainly made a good job of it. She had run right up on to the reef she had struck, and

now lay tilted drunkenly over on her port side, with her forward part right out of the water. Huge waves were sweeping her amidships.

Captain Proctor made a circuit of her. She was lifting and lurching as the waves pounded her, and she had a very tall mast which was whipping viciously back and forth with her movement. He knew that if he got too near that, it would be the end of him and his crew, and quite possibly the end for all those people down there. He could see them quite clearly, clustered as far away from the surging seas as they could get, hanging on for their lives. With the ship at that angle and moving the way she was, it was obviously quite impossible for them to stand.

Captain Proctor completed his reconnaissance and came to a hover at a height of about fifty metres, with the ship on his starboard beam. Just to stay in one place was difficult enough, and he needed that much height to keep clear of the mast.

Sergeant Monnie looked down at the ship. It seemed a long way below him. There was very little clear deck space, and a small area towards the stern seemed to him to be the best place from which to take people off. He said as much to Captain Proctor, and the captain agreed.

Landing or even descending any further was out of the question, so they were going to lower a rescue basket. Even that was going to be frighteningly difficult. From that height the hoist cable, especially with the basket on the end catching the wind, would be blown a long way out of the vertical. That was not all. In addition to her high mast, the Arnel seemed to have more than her fair share of rigging. If the basket got entangled in that . . . But they had to have a go. There were all those lives at stake down there.

'O.K., Monnie?' Captain Proctor said. 'Lower away!'

Sergeant Monnie began to lower the basket on the winch fitted in the helicopter for that purpose. His was just as vital a function in the rescue operation as the pilot's. From his seat at the controls, Captain Proctor could not see the ship and had to rely on directions from the hoist operator.

The basket drifted down on a long, wind-blown arc of cable. The clear space it was being aimed at looked like a postage stamp.

'Back now,' Sergeant Monnie said. 'Back ... back! Hold it! That's good. Now forward a little ...'

The basket had almost reached the deck, but it was drifting out over the side of the ship. On Sergeant Monnie's instructions, Captain Proctor made further minute adjustments to the helicopter's position, and the basket came down right on target.

Sergeant Monnie saw figures round the basket, holding it. They didn't appear to be doing anything else.

'Come on – come on!' Monnie muttered under his breath. 'We haven't got all night!'

'What's going on down there?' Captain Proctor said.

Someone was getting into the basket.

'They're taking their time,' Monnie said. And then, suddenly, 'O.K.! We got one!'

In point of fact they'd got two. The first survivors of the *Arnel* to be lifted off in the rescue basket were a woman and her baby.

The helicopter flew them a short distance to high ground on the edge of the island, where other rescuers were waiting to take care of them. It then returned to the wreck to repeat the process.

The *Arnel* operation was an extraordinary test of endurance as well as skill. Except for the mothers with their babies, it was a question of lifting off one person at a time. Each time the helicopter had to be talked into position, the basket drifted over the wreck, and the 'catch' hoisted and flown to safety.

The seven women and three children on the ship were naturally given priority. They were flown ashore first, and then the helicopter had to return to base to refuel. While this was being done, Captain Proctor asked the Portuguese authorities to write a note to the captain of the *Arnel* requesting him to have the high mast which was threatening the rescue operation taken down. The helicopter was going to drop the note when it got back to the wreck, but in fact when it did return, the *Arnel's* skipper had anticipated the request. The mast was being dismantled – in itself a perilous operation.

The lift-off was technically much easier once the mast was down, but set against that was the length of time the operation was taking. Captain Proctor and his co-pilot were becoming exhausted with the effort of maintaining a precise position in gale-force conditions. The rudder controls were operated by the feet, and the constant pressure required was particularly hard on the legs. Sergeant Monnie's role was just as taxing in a different way. By the time it was all over, he had been 'talking' the rescue basket down and up again for a total of four and a half hours.

They never faltered in their dangerous task, and by nightfall all the forty-eight people on the *Arnel* had been airlifted to safety by that one 'whirlybird' with its crew of three. The operation had gone so smoothly that two of the babies didn't even wake up! The three Americans' skill, courage and endurance was recognised by their own country by the award of the D.F.C. (Distinguished Flying Cross) to Captain Proctor and Air Medals to Lieutenant Gagnon and Sergeant Monnie.

The helicopter only reached a useful stage of development during the latter part of World War Two, and it is thought that its first employment in a rescue operation at sea occurred when two men were lifted off an oil barge which had run aground in a gale on the Atlantic coast of the U.S.A. – much the same situation as in the case of the *Arnel*, except that the locale was different. From then on helicopters came rapidly and dramatically into their own as rescue machines. Nowadays many thousands of people are saved every year in all parts of the world by this lifeline in the sky.

The Ditch

He dived behind one of the Messerschmitts and opened fire at two hundred metres. His Spitfire checked and juddered violently as the cannon shells streamed out from her. He watched the apparently lazy way they curved towards the target. Nearer and nearer . . .

He never knew whether any of them hit, because within seconds he had become a target himself. Another Messerschmitt which he hadn't seen was coming in from his starboard side. All at once his windscreen was covered with a thick film of oil.

It happened just after noon one Wednesday in June, 1941, when the struggle for air supremacy between Britain and Germany in World War Two was at its height. He had been on a fighter sweep over occupied France and was roughly halfway between the big industrial town of Lille and the French coast on his way back when he was hit.

Luckily the second Messerschmitt hadn't pressed home its attack, but he was still in a pretty bad spot. After another kilometre or so his engine was already overheating and beginning to run roughly. It was obvious he wasn't going to get home.

He had to make up his mind what to do – and make it up quickly. If he landed in France he would almost certainly be taken prisoner and be out of the war for good. At best it would be a long time before he flew again, and, after what had happened that day, he couldn't wait to get his own back! On the other hand, he hadn't a hope of getting back across the Channel. Not in the air, anyway. He made his decision. If he couldn't get home, he'd get as near as he possibly could.

The Spitfire's engine had a horrible grating sound to it now. Then, suddenly, it stopped, completely seized up. By that time he was too low to bale out even if he'd wanted to. He was near the

French coast, so he decided to fly out over it and land on the sea. Luckily it was a fine, calm day.

He pancaked the plane as carefully as he could, but overdid it a bit. The Spitfire made first contact with the water with its tail, and almost immediately afterwards tipped up on its nose and went down like a stone.

He went down with it. On impact something hit him hard across the eyes, and after that he couldn't see. He struggled to get out of the plane's cramped little cockpit but found himself held down by the straps of the parachute he was sitting on. A parachute was about the last thing he needed now! The thing that might in other circumstances have saved his life now seemed bent on drowning him.

The Spitfire was still plummetting down towards the sea bed, and he was trapped inside it. He felt sure he wasn't going to get out, and that this was the end of everything for him.

He made another frantic effort to escape – and suddenly he was free. He was out of the plane. It seemed to take him for ever to reach the surface, and his lungs were bursting by the time he did get there. But he'd made it! All at once he was gasping down great draughts of the most wonderful fresh air he had ever breathed.

The parachute continued to hamper him. He still had the harness on, and it was dragging at him. He shrugged himself out of it.

Now he was swimming free in a calm blue sea, with the afternoon summer sun beating down on him. He rubbed his hand across his eyes and, when he looked at it, saw blood. But at least he could see.

He also saw the pack which contained his emergency dinghy floating a little way away from him. He swam to it and pulled the string which operated the compressed gas bottle. The dinghy unfolded and filled. He felt a surge of relief as the little boat took shape. It was very small, but it was a boat none the less. It would keep him afloat. All he had to do was get into it and wait to be rescued.

But getting into it was easier said than done. He tried three times, but the boat was so light that each time his weight pushed one side down under the surface while the other shot up in the air. Then he remembered the water-pocket in the nose which was designed for this very purpose – when filled, it would act as a counterweight.

Remembering the drill for filling the water-pocket, he pushed the dinghy forward, and was overwhelmed with pleasure and a sense of achievement when he found that this enabled him to get aboard quite easily over the stern.

The sun was still shining brightly, and looked like going on doing so. The sky was cloudless, and the sea as calm as a pond. He couldn't have chosen a better day to 'ditch'!

But it would have been better still if he hadn't had to – if he had got back from the mission safe and sound. It was still only about 1 p.m. Back on the station they would be having a beer or two and thinking about lunch in the mess. He could certainly do with a drink himself!

He spent a few minutes trying to paddle the dinghy away from France and towards England, but soon realised that would literally get him nowhere. But the English Channel was a busy thoroughfare, both on the water and in the air above it. He'd be bound to be spotted before very long – and meanwhile his clothes were drying out nicely.

The afternoon wore away. The circle of blue sea of which he was the tiny centre remained empty of other craft, but there was a lot happening overhead. There was scarcely a minute when he couldn't hear the sound of aircraft. He couldn't see them, but that was probably because of the injury he had received. He no longer had blood in his eyes, but he couldn't see anything very clearly.

It was mid-evening when he resigned himself to a night in the dinghy. The aerial activity had stopped for the time being – no doubt the 'night shift' would be on later – and, though it was still full daylight, a haze was forming over the surface of the sea, limiting visibility to a few hundred metres. No one was going to spot him now.

Gradually it grew dark, and, as it did so, a small, chill breeze blew up. The dinghy began to ship water. The sea was by no means rough, but the little air-boat was only the length of a man, and its sides were only twenty centimetres high. Even wavelets slopped into it.

It was a very long night, or so it seemed to him. Although it was summer, he got very cold. The dinghy was far too small for him to take any kind of exercise. He lay shivering, soaked to the skin, waiting for the dawn.

It came at last, and luckily it heralded another fine, sunny day. As soon as the sun was high enough to have any warmth in it, he took off his clothes and spread them out to dry. Even that wasn't an easy operation. More than once he almost tipped himself and his things over the side.

He had got into a strange state of mind by now. Cold, the discomfort of wet clothes, lack of food and drink, plus the shock, both physical and mental, of the ditching the day before, had combined to make him drowsy and not very interested in what was happening to him. None of it seemed in any way real.

He dozed on and off all day, again hearing aircraft much of the time without being able to see them.

Then, towards evening, he was shaken out of his lethargy when he spotted a boat. It was the size of a small motor launch, and for a moment or two his spirits soared at the sight of it. He never doubted that it was coming to pick him up.

Then he realised that it wasn't moving – and, what was more, that it was German. It was a boat of the kind both the Germans and the British moored off their coasts to provide temporary safety and shelter for any of their airmen who had had to ditch or bale out in the vicinity.

German or not, the boat represented a warm, dry place with food and drink, to say nothing of safety from the sea. He started paddling towards it, and after a while realised that he wasn't going to get there. In spite of his efforts, the boat was further away than it had been when he'd first caught sight of it. It became smaller and smaller as the dinghy drifted away, until it disappeared altogether.

That night and the following day were repetitions of the first. At dusk a light breeze started to blow and the sea got up – only a little, but enough to soak him through in a matter of minutes. At dawn the sun rose in a cloudless sky, and an hour or two later he stripped off and dried his clothes, not so successfully this time because by now they were getting sticky and stiff with salt. He frequently heard aircraft but never saw one, and none of them saw him.

His strange, detached mood persisted, but he hadn't yet given up hope of coming through his ordeal alive. When, at about seven o'clock that evening, he saw another moored refuge launch, he made up his mind that somehow or other he was going to get to it. A tremendous additional spur this time was that this boat was British.

It was no good trying to paddle towards it – he'd proved that last time. Instead he slipped into the sea, tied the straps of his lifejacket to the dinghy, and set off to swim to the launch, towing the little rubber boat behind him.

He'd covered perhaps a kilometre when he realised, as he had before, that he wasn't going to make it. He'd done superbly well to swim even that distance in his weakened state, but now he could do no more. It was almost more than he could manage to get back into the dinghy. After a tremendous effort he hauled himself over the side and collapsed into it just as the sun was setting.

He had now been adrift in his frail little inflatable boat, no bigger than an air-bed, for two whole days and nights.

His third night was worse than either of the previous two. The cycle he had come to dread was repeated, with the wind and sea getting up at dusk, except that this time the wind was stronger and the sea correspondingly rougher. Worse still, this time, after his recent immersion, he hadn't even the temporary comfort of starting off with dry clothes. For really good measure, it rained.

He sometimes thought afterwards that it was only the sun that kept him going. Next morning it shone as brightly as ever. Wearily, almost in a daze, he took off his clothes to dry them.

By this time he was beginning to suffer badly from thirst. He wasn't in the least hungry, but he craved a long, cool drink. His throat felt caked and sore with salt. He thought longingly of the many pleasant hours he'd spent in the station mess drinking beer with his friends. If only they could see him now! If only *someone* could see him!

That morning hundreds of aircraft flew over him, heading for France, but he could scarcely rouse himself to take any interest in them. He was convinced by this time that unless some plane or other flew very low and immediately over him, he would never be spotted.

At about one o'clock that afternoon a large formation passed overhead, and this time he not only heard the planes but saw them. He was even able to identify them as Blenheim bombers. They disappeared in the direction of the French coast without seeing him.

He waited for them to come back. There was no reason why they should fly right over him again, or, even if they did, any more chance of their seeing him. All the same, he couldn't help feeling more excited and hopeful than he had done at any time before.

They did come back. Again he heard them before he saw them, and could tell from their engine noise that they were flying low. When they came in sight, they were only a few hundred metres up. They flew past him at a distance of about a kilometre without seeing him.

His excitement evaporated. He wasn't really surprised, or even disappointed. He had been a fool to expect anything different. It was only what had happened before, and would doubtless happen again.

Then he heard more engine noise, though much less in volume this time. Shortly afterwards two aircraft came into view, one of them a Blenheim and the other a fighter – a Hurricane – which was escorting the bomber.

Both planes were very low, and they were flying straight towards him. He waved frantically, as he had done so many times before, but they flew straight on without deviating a centimetre from their course. Then, when they were well past him, both planes banked, and he knew they *had* seen him!

After a good, long look, the Blenheim flew on, but the Hurricane stayed behind, flying round and round him. That plane was the most wonderful sight he had ever seen in the whole of his life.

It seemed a long time after that before anything further happened, but actually it was only a little over half an hour later when a Lysander appeared, escorted by three Spitfires. The Lysander was a spotting aircraft, used, among other things, for observation and gunnery control. Because of its very low stalling speed it could pinpoint an object more accurately than most other planes.

The Lysander took over from the Hurricane and flew in a close circle round the dinghy. He lay on his back in the little boat, feeling very weak now.

Not long afterwards he saw the most welcome sight of all – an Air Sea Rescue launch speeding towards him. It reduced speed as it approached, then put its engines astern and edged carefully alongside the dinghy. He thought that all he'd got to do then was climb aboard the launch, and made an effort to do so, only to find that he couldn't even stand up. Two of the crew of the launch reached over the side and pulled him aboard.

They took him below decks. He was shivering, and the first thing the skipper of the launch did was to pour him a glass of rum to warm him up. But then, in the act of handing him the glass, the skipper said, 'Wait a minute. When did you last eat?'

He tried to work it out, but he couldn't count up the days. All he knew was what day it had been when he'd flown his last mission. He replied, his voice a hoarse croak, 'Wednesday.'

'Good God!' the launch's skipper exclaimed. 'It's Sunday today!'

So they gave him a glass of water with just a trace of rum in it. They made him lie down for a while, and later gave him a slice of plain bread, then another with butter and jam on it, followed by another glass of water, and another of rum and water mixed. He was sure he'd never known anything so wonderful as just drinking.

Meanwhile the launch was speeding back to the English coast. It put him ashore at a port in Kent where an ambulance was waiting to take him to hospital. There it was discovered that the facial injury which had affected his sight wasn't serious, and that there was nothing else wrong with him that rest and nourishment wouldn't cure. Within a fortnight he was flying again.

This pilot's story is typical of what happened to many of the brave young men, Winston Churchill's 'few', who fought in the air to defend Britain and the free world against the might of Hitler's Germany, and who, by their gallantry, won a great victory.

There were others too, who, though the part they played wasn't quite so dramatic, made an important contribution to that victory.

Among them were the crew of the Air Sea Rescue launch which picked up our pilot, and who were at sea again within the hour, speeding to the rescue of another airman who had been forced to 'ditch' in the Channel.

The Air Sea Rescue Service came into being between the two world wars. To start with it was merely a collection of small vessels primarily concerned with rescue work connected with flying boat exercises. Then, with the build-up to another war in the late 1930s, a number of high-speed launches were built. They were nineteen metres long and had very powerful engines. When World War Two broke out in 1939, there were nine of these craft stationed around Britain, and four more overseas.

As the war at sea and in the air intensified, a rapid build-up followed. During the course of World War Two, the Air Sea Rescue Service saved a total of 13,269 lives, including 8,604 aircrew.

More Beaver Books

We hope you have enjoyed this Beaver Book. Here are some of the other titles:

Ghostly and Ghastly A Beaver original. Thirteen stories of ghostly happenings collected by Barbara Ireson and illustrated by William Geldart make a spine-chilling read for everyone from nine upwards

My Favourite Escape Stories Pat Reid, author of *The Colditz Story*, presents his favourite true stories from four hundred years of escapes. Gripping reading for everyone from nine upwards

Wild Lone 'BB's' classic depiction of the life of a fox in hunting countryside, for older readers. The author's book *The Lord of the Forest* is also available in Beavers

Storm Warning A powerful novel for older readers set in pre-war Nazi Germany, about a young English girl who helps two Jewish children escape from the Gestapo. By Mara Kay

Sizing up Science Written by R. Houwink and illustrated throughout, this book brings scientific facts and figures vividly to life in a comprehensible and often amusing manner

Air Quiz A Beaver original. Questions on flying, from the early days of balloons to supersonic planes and space rockets, by J. E. Thompson. Illustrated throughout by John Batchelor

New Beavers are published every month and if you would like the *Beaver Bulletin* – which gives all the details – please send a large stamped addressed envelope to:

Beaver Bulletin
The Hamlyn Group
Astronaut House
Feltham
Middlesex TW14 9AR

382397